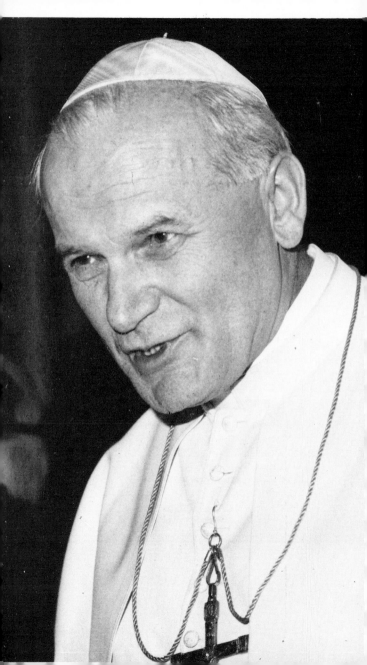

VISIBLE SIGNS OF THE GOSPEL

Messages of John Paul II on Consecrated Life

Compiled and Indexed
by the
Daughters of St. Paul

ST. PAUL EDITIONS

Reprinted with permission from *L'Osservatore Romano*, English Edition.

ISBN 0-8198-8000-0 (cloth)
ISBN 0-8198-8001-9 (paper)

cover photo: Media Center

Printed in U.S.A. by the Daughters of St. Paul
50 St. Paul's Ave., Boston, Ma. 02130

The Daughters of St. Paul are an international congregation of religious women serving the Church with the communications media.

CONTENTS

Fidelity to Vatican Council II

On the morning of October 17, 1978, the day after his election as Supreme Pontiff, Pope John Paul II celebrated Mass together with the College of Cardinals in the Sistine Chapel. At the end of the Mass, His Holiness spoke to the Cardinals and to the world. Excerpts follow.

...As the Council is not limited to the documents alone, neither is it completed by the ways of applying it which were devised in these post-conciliar years. Therefore, we rightly consider that we are bound by the primary duty of most diligently furthering the implementation of the decrees and directive norms of that same Universal Synod. This indeed we shall do in a way that is at once prudent and stimulating. We shall strive, in particular, that first of all an appropriate mentality may flourish. Namely, it is necessary that, above all, outlooks must be at one with the Council so that in practice those things may be done that were ordered by it, and that those things which lie hidden in it or—as is usually said—are "implicit," may become explicit in the light of the experiments made since then and the demands of changing circumstances. Briefly, it is necessary that the fertile seeds which the Fathers of the Ecumenical Synod, nourished by the Word of God, sowed in good ground (cf. Mt. 13:8, 23)—that is, the important teachings and pastoral deliberations—should be brought to maturity in that way which is characteristic of movement and life.

This general purpose of fidelity to the Second Vatican Council and the express will, insofar as we are concerned, of bringing it into effect, can cover various sections: missionary and ecumenical affairs, discipline, and suitable administration. But there is one section to which greater attention will have to be given, and that is the ecclesiological section. Venerable brethren and beloved sons of the Catholic world, it is necessary for us to take once again into our hands the "Magna Charta" of the Council, that is, the Dogmatic Constitution *Lumen gentium,* so that with renewed and invigorating zeal we may meditate on the nature and function of the Church, its way of being and acting. This should be done not merely in order that the vital communion in Christ of all who believe and hope in Him should be accomplished, but also in order to contribute to bringing about a fuller and closer unity of the whole human family.

Beloved brothers in the episcopate and dear children, fidelity, as is clear, implies not a wavering obedience to the magisterium of Peter, especially in what pertains to doctrine. The "objective" importance of this magisterium must always be kept in mind and even safeguarded because of the attacks which in our time are being leveled here and there against certain truths of the Catholic Faith. Fidelity too implies the observance of the liturgical norms laid down by ecclesiastical authority and therefore has nothing to do with the practice either of introducing innovations of one's own accord and without approval or of obstinately refusing to carry out what has been lawfully laid down and introduced into the

Riches of Living Faith
at the Heart of the Church

Over twelve thousand sisters resident in Rome took part in the meeting with the Holy Father on November 10, 1978.

At the beginning of the audience, Cardinal Poletti delivered an address of homage to the Holy Father, to which John Paul II replied with the following discourse.

Dear sisters,

1. Yesterday, on the festivity of the dedication of the Basilica of the Holy Savior in the Lateran, I began the preparation for the great act of taking possession of this Basilica—the Cathedral of the Bishop of Rome—which will take place next Sunday. For this reason I met yesterday the clergy of the diocese of Rome, the priests engaged particularly in the diocesan apostolate. Today I meet you, sisters. I wanted this meeting to follow yesterday's immediately. Thus, as new Bishop of Rome, I can approach those who contitute, in a certain way, the principal spiritual reserves of this diocese, the first among all the iioceses in the Church, and I can have at least a first contact with them. This approach and this acquaintance are of great concern to me.

LARGE MEMBERSHIP

You have come here in very large numbers! Perhaps no episcopal See in the world can count so many. The Cardinal Vicar of Rome has informed me that in the territory of the diocese there are about 20,000 religious women, about 200 generalates, and about 500 provincial houses of various female orders and congregations. These houses are in the service of your religious families in the range of the whole Church, or of the provinces, which go beyond the territory of the city of Rome. During the years of my episcopal ministry, I often met the female orders (Krakow is the richest in them in Poland), and I had the opportunity to realize how much each congregation wishes to have a house, and above all the generalate, right in Rome, near the Pope. I rejoice in this and thank you, even if I am of the opinion that you should always remain faithful to your birthplace, where the motherhouse is, where the light of the new community, of the new vocation, of the new mission in the Church appeared for the first time.

2. I welcome all of you sisters gathered here today. I wish to greet you in the first place as the new Bishop of Rome and I wish to specify your place in this "local Church," in this actual diocese, of which I am preparing to take possession solemnly next Sunday. Judging by the living centuries-old tradition of the Church, by the recent doctrine of the Second Vatican Council and also by my previous experiences as a bishop, I come here with the deep conviction that this is a special "place."

FREEDOM OF THE SPIRIT

This is seen from the vision of man and of his vocation which Christ Himself expressed to us. *"Qui potest capere, capiat"* (Mt. 19:12) ("He who is able to receive this, let him receive it"); thus He spoke to His disciples who were asking Him insistent questions on the legislation of the Old Testament and especially on the legislation regarding marriage. In these questions, as also in the tradition of the Old Testament, there was included a certain limitation of that freedom of children of God which Christ brought us, and which St. Paul, subsequently, confirmed so forcefully. The religious vocation is precisely the fruit of this freedom of spirit, reawakened by Christ, from which there springs the availability of complete giving to God Himself. The religious vocation lies in the acceptance of a severe discipline, which does not come from an order, but from an evangelical counsel: the counsel of chastity, the counsel of poverty, the counsel of obedience. And all that, embraced consciously and rooted in love for the divine Bridegroom, is, in fact, the particular revelation of the depth of the freedom of the human spirit. Freedom of the children of God: sons and daughters.

This vocation is derived from a living faith, consistent with the ultimate consequences, which opens up to man the final perspective, that is, the perspective of the meeting with God Himself, who alone is worthy of a love "above everything," an exclusive and nuptial love. This love consists in the giving of our whole human being, body and soul, to Him who gave Himself completely to us men by means of the Incarnation, the cross and abasement, by means of poverty, chastity, obedience: He became poor for us...so that we might become rich (cf. 2 Cor. 8:9). In this way, therefore, the religious vocation takes life from these riches of living faith. This vocation is, as it were, the spark which lights a "bright flame of love" in the soul, as St. John of the Cross wrote. This vocation, once accepted, once solemnly confirmed by means of the vows, must continually be nourished by the riches of faith; not only when it brings with it inner joy, but also when it is accompanied by difficulties, aridity, and inner suffering, which is called the "night" of the soul.

RENDERING SERVICE

This vocation is a special treasure of the Church, which can never cease to pray that the Spirit of Jesus Christ will bring forth religious vocations in souls. They are, in fact, both for the community of the People of God, and for the "world," a living sign of the "future life": a sign which, at the same time, is rooted (also by means of your religious habit) in the everyday life of the Church and of society, and permeates its most delicate tissues. The persons who have loved God unreservedly are particularly capable of loving man, and of giving themselves to him without personal interests and without limits. Do we need proofs? We can find them in every age of the Church's life; we find them also in our times. During my preceding episcopal ministry, I met such testimonies at every step. I remember the institutes and hospitals for the seriously ill and for the handicapped. Everywhere, in places where no one could render service as a good Samaritan any longer, there was always still a sister to be found.

GO OUT TO OTHERS

This is certainly only one of the fields of activity, and therefore only an example. These fields are certainly far more numerous, in actual fact. Well, meeting you here today, for the first time, dear sisters, I wish to tell you in the first place that your presence is indispensable in the whole Church, and especially here in Rome, in this diocese. It must be a visible sign of the Gospel for all. It must also be the source of a particular apostolate. This apostolate is so varied and rich that it is even difficult for me to list here all its forms, its fields, its orientations. It is united with the specific charism of every congregation, with its apostolic spirit, which the Church and the Holy See approve with joy, seeing in it the expression of the vitality of the Mystical Body of Christ! This apostolate is usually discreet, hidden, near to the human being, and so is more suited to a woman's soul, sensitive to her neighbor, and hence called to the task of a sister and mother. It is precisely this vocation which is at the very "heart" of your religious being. As Bishop of Rome I beg you: be spiritually mothers and sisters for all the people of this Church which Jesus, in His ineffable mercy and grace, has wished to entrust to me. Be it for everyone, without exception, but especially for the sick, the suffering, the abandoned, the children, the young, families in difficult situations.... Go out towards them! Do not wait for them to come to you! Look for them yourselves! Love drives us to do so. Love must seek! *Caritas Christi urget nos*—"The love of Christ drives us!" (2 Cor. 5:14)

GENEROUS COMMITMENT

And I entrust to you another request at the beginning of this pastoral ministry of mine: commit yourselves generously to collaborating with the grace of God, in order that so many young souls may accept the Lord's call and new forces come to swell your ranks, to meet the growing requirements that are emerging in the vast fields of the modern apostolate. The first form of collaboration is certainly assiduous invocation to "the Lord of the harvest" (cf. Mt. 9:38) to enlighten and guide the hearts of the many girls "in quest" who certainly exist, today too, in this diocese, as in every part of the world. May they understand that there is no greater ideal to which to dedicate their lives than that of the complete gift of themselves to Christ for the service of the kingdom. But there is a second way, no less important, of assisting God's call, and it is that of the witness that emanates from your lives:

—the witness, in the first place, of sincere consistency with Gospel values and with the specific charism of your institute: any surrender to compromise is a disappointment for those who approach you, do not forget!

—the witness, moreover, of a harmonious and mature personality, which is able to establish relations with others without unjustified prejudices or ingenuous imprudence, but with cordial openness and serene balance;

—the witness, finally, of your joy, a joy that can be read in your eyes and in your attitude as well as in your words; a joy which clearly manifests, to those who look at you, awareness of possessing that "hidden treasure," that "pearl of great value," the purchase of which takes away all regret at having renounced everything in accordance with the evangelical counsel (cf. Mt. 13:44-45).

"I WILL BE LOVE"

And now, before concluding, I wish to address a special word to the dear enclosed sisters, to those present at this meeting and to those who are in their austere enclosure, chosen for a special love of the divine Bridegroom. I greet you all with particular intensity of sentiments, and in spirit I visit your convents, apparently closed, but actually so deeply open to the presence of God living in our human world, and therefore so necessary for the world. I commend to you the Church and Rome; I commend to you men and the world! To you, to your prayers, to your "holocaust." I commend also myself, Bishop of Rome. Be with me, close to me, you who are "in the heart of the Church"! May there be fulfilled in each of you that which was the program of life for St. Thérèse of the Child Jesus: *in corde ecclesiae amor ero*—"I will be love in the heart of the Church!"

In this way, I end my first meeting with the sisters of holy Rome. In you continues the extraordinary sowing of the Gospel, the extraordinary expression of that call to holiness which the Council recently recalled to us in the Constitution on the Church. I expect a great deal from you. I place great hopes in you. I wish to enclose and express all this in the blessing which I willingly impart to you.

I commend you to Mary, the Bride of the Holy Spirit, the Mother of the noblest love!

"Be True Daughters of the Church, not Only in Words but in Deeds"

At the conclusion of the annual session of the International Union of Mothers General, about six hundred women religious belonging to the Union were received in audience by the Holy Father on November 16, 1978.

Pope John Paul II delivered the following address.

Dear sisters,

Ecce quam bonum et iucundum habitare fratres in unum.... You love this psalm and you are living it at this moment. The time when religious congregations met but little, for geographical reasons and others perhaps, is practically over. God be praised! And congratulations to you, too, my sisters: you bear witness, in various ways, to one treasure entrusted by Christ Himself to His Church: the incomparable treasure of the evangelical counsels!

Certainly, your International Union of Mothers General is just emerging from infancy. It is only thirteen years old! But it has already yielded good fruit. The new Pope, like his very deserving predecessor, Paul VI, who received you so many times, would like it to yield even more. The famous parable of the vine and the vinedresser must often be present to my spirit and yours (Jn. 15:1-8).

Your meeting has as its subject "Religious Life and New Mankind." It is a fundamental subject, a very old one and very relevant today. Though the whole People of God is called to become a new mankind in Christ and through Christ (Constitution *Lumen gentium,* ch. 5), the ways of access to this new mankind, in other words to holiness, are different and must remain so. Precisely chapter six of *Lumen gentium,* without making the least discrimination among members of the People of God which would contradict the redeeming plan of Christ Jesus—a plan of holiness and unity for the world—always illumines your way.

"LET US FIRST BE CHRISTIANS"

Since the Council, the religious congregations have in fact multiplied the times and the means of deepening essential religious values. They have rightly put them back into the wake of the primary, ontological, ineffaceable consecration which is baptism. And all sisters have, as it were, conveyed to one another a password: "Let us first be Christians!"—a certain number preferring or adding the following: "Let us first be women!" It is evident that the two do not exclude each other. These striking formulas have found a favorable echo in a large part of the People of God. But the positive side of this awareness cannot dispense from continuous and prudent vigilance. The treasure of the evangelical counsels and the commitment—taken after mature reflection and irrevocable—to make them the charter of a Christian existence cannot be relativized by public opinion, even if it were ecclesial. The Church and, let us say, the world itself need, more than ever, men and women who sacrifice everything to follow Christ in the way of the Apostles. And to such an extent that the sacrifice of conjugal love, of material possessions, of the completely autonomous exercise of freedom, becomes incomprehensible without love of Christ.

OBLIGATION TO BEAR WITNESS

This radicalism is necessary to proclaim prophetically, but always very humbly, this new mankind according to Christ, completely available for God and completely available for other men. Every woman religious must bear witness to the primacy of God and must dedicate a sufficiently long period of time every day to stand before the Lord, to tell Him her love, and above all to let herself be loved by Him. Every woman religious must signify every day, by her way of life, that she chooses simplicity and poor means for everything that concerns her personal and community life. Every woman religious must do God's will and not her own every day, to signify that human plans, hers and those of society, are not the only plans in history, but that there exists a plan of God which calls for the sacrifice of one's own freedom. This real prophetic element of the evangelical counsels, lived day after day, and altogether possible with the grace of God, is not a proud lesson given to the Christian people.

It is a light absolutely indispensable for the life of the Church—which is sometimes tempted to have recourse to the means of power—and even indispensable for mankind wandering along the alluring and disappointing paths of materialism and atheism.

And if your consecration to God is really such a deep reality, it is not unimportant to bear permanently its exterior sign which a simple and suitable religious habit constitutes: it is the means to remind yourselves constantly of your commitment which contrasts strongly with the spirit of the world; it is a silent but eloquent testimony; it is a sign that our secularized world needs to find on its way, as many Christians, moreover, desire. I ask you to turn this over carefully in your minds.

That is, my sisters, the price of your realistic participation in the proclamation and the building up of this "new mankind." For man cannot be fully satisfied—beyond earthly goods, necessary for his life and, alas, so badly shared out—except by knowledge and love of God, inseparable from acceptance and love of all men, especially the poorest on the human and moral plane. All the efforts, all the transformations of your congregations, must be carried out in this perspective, otherwise you are working in vain!

LOVE THE CHURCH

All that, my sisters, is the ideal towards which you are striving personally, and towards which you draw along your companions of the evangelical way in a motherly and firm manner. In practice, you know it better than others, from time to time you come up against unavoidable contingencies: either the rapid social changes in a country, or the small number and aging of your subjects, or again the wind of interminable researches and experiments, the requests of the young, etc.... Accept all these realities. Take them seriously, never tragically. Seek calmly for progressive, clear and courageous solutions. While remaining yourselves, seek with others. Above all, be daughters of the Church, not only in words but in deeds! In ever-renewed faithfulness to the charism of their founders, the congregations must, in fact, endeavor to meet the expectations of the Church and the commitments which the Church, with her pastors, consider most urgent today in order to face up to a mission which needs skilled workers so much. A guarantee of this exemplary love of the Church—inseparable from love of Christ Jesus—is your dialogue with those in charge of your local Churches, with a resolution of faithfulness and devotion to these Churches; also a guarantee are your trustful relations with our Congregation for Religious and for Secular Institutes. Dear sisters, the capital of generosity of your congregations is immense. Use these forces responsibly. Do not allow them to be scattered thoughtlessly.

THE POPE'S AFFECTION

I ask you to express to each of your sisters, whatever her place may be in the congregation for which you are responsible, the Pope's affection but also the hope that he sets in her for the renewal of an exacting practice of the evangelical counsels, for the significant witness of all religious communities whose ardent faith, apostolic inspiration and, of course, interpersonal relations would make those who are seeking new ways in our society, harassed by materialism, violence and fear, say: "we have found a model to imitate...." Yes, my sisters, in the Church herself, in the footsteps of St. Catherine of Siena and of St. Teresa of Avila, among so many others, you can show the place that is due to woman.

May the Holy Spirit act powerfully in you! With Mary, who was perfectly docile to Him, live listening to God's Word and put it into practice, unto the cross. May your complete gift to Christ always be a source of joy, dynamism and peace! To all of you, to all of those whom you represent, our apostolic blessing.

Full Ecclesial Communion in a Spirit of True Charity

On November 23, 1978, Pope John Paul II received a group of bishops of Honduras for their visit "ad limina Apostolorum." His Holiness delivered an address, of which the following is an excerpt.

Let us not forget the irreplaceable and specific place that priests have in the sanctification of the People of God, appointed as they are by the Lord "to hold in the community of the faithful the sacred power of Order, that of offering sacrifice and forgiving sins, and to exercise the priestly office publicly on behalf of men in the name of Christ" (Decree on the Ministry of Priests, no. 2).

It is a question of vital importance for the Church. From it is derived the precise duty of giving absolute priority to the fostering of vocations to the priesthood, and likewise to the consecrated life. It is a great task which must be undertaken with all diligence, with the subsequent training of those who have been called, to a strong sense of faith and service for the world today.

To create an environment propitious to the flourishing of vocations, the ecclesial community will have to offer a testimony of life in conformity with the essential values of the Gospel. In this way they will be able to arouse generous souls, directed towards complete commitment to Christ and others, with confidence in the Lord and in the reward promised to those who serve Him faithfully.

Religious Life as a Way to Salvation

On November 24, 1978, John Paul II received in audience 90 male Superiors General, accompanied by Cardinal Eduardo Pironio, Prefect of the Sacred Congregation for Religious and for Secular Institutes. The Holy Father delivered the following address.

Beloved sons,

1. This is my first opportunity to meet the Superiors General of the male orders, a meeting to which I attach particular importance. When I see you gathered here, there appear before my eyes magnificent figures of saints, the great saints who gave rise to your religious families: Basil, Augustine, Benedict, Dominic, Francis, Ignatius of Loyola, Francis de Sales, Vincent de Paul, John-Baptist de La Salle, Paul of the Cross, Alphonsus Liguori. And then, nearer to us, there are Joseph Benedict Cottolengo, John Bosco, Vincent Pallotti; not to speak of the most recent ones, whose holiness still awaits the definitive judgment of the Church, but whose beneficial influence is testified by the host of generous souls who have chosen to follow their example.

FOUNDER'S CHARISM

All these names—and I have mentioned only some—bear witness that the ways of holiness, to which the members of the People of God are called, passed and still pass, to a great extent,

through the religious life. This should not sur-
prise us, since religious life is based on the most
precise "recipe" for holiness, which is constituted by love realized according to the evangelical counsels.

Furthermore, each of your founders, under
the inspiration of the Holy Spirit, promised by
Christ to the Church, was a man who possessed a
particular charism. Christ had in him an exceptional "instrument" for His work of salvation,
which especially in this way is perpetuated in the
history of the human family. The Church has
gradually assumed these charisms, evaluated
them and, when she found them authentic,
thanked the Lord for them and tried to "put
them in a safe place" in the life of the community, so that they could always yield fruit.

This was recalled by the Second Vatican
Council, which stressed how the ecclesiastical
hierarchy, on which there falls the task of feeding
the People of God and leading them to good pastures, "in docile response to the promptings of
the Holy Spirit accepts rules of religious life
which are presented for its approval by outstanding men and women, improves them further and
then officially authorizes them. It uses its super-
visory and protective authority, too, to ensure
that religious institutes established all over the
world for building up the Body of Christ may
develop and flourish in accordance with the
spirit of their founders" (Dogmatic Constitution
Lumen gentium, no. 45, 1).

This is what I desire first of all to recognize
and express during our first meeting. I do not in-

tend here to make reference "to the past," understood as a historical period that is concluded in
itself; I intend to refer "to the life" of the Church
in her deepest dynamics. To her life, as it is
presented before us *today*, bringing with it the
riches of the traditions of the past, to offer us the
possibility of taking advantage of them *today*.

VERTICAL DIMENSION
TAKES PRIORITY

2. The religious vocation is a great problem
of the Church of our time. For this very reason it
is necessary in the first place to reaffirm forcefully that it belongs to that spiritual fullness which
the Spirit Himself—the Spirit of Christ—brings
forth and molds in the People of God. Without
religious orders, without "consecrated" life by
means of the vows of chastity, poverty and obedience, the Church would not be fully herself. Religious, in fact, "at the deepest level of their being
are caught up in the dynamism of the Church's
life, which is thirsty for the divine Absolute and
called to holiness. It is to this holiness that they
bear witness. They embody the Church in her
desire to give herself completely to the radical
demands of the beatitudes. By their lives they are
a sign of total availability to God, the Church and
the brethren" (Apostolic Exhortation *Evangelii
nuntiandi*, no. 69).

Accepting this axiom, we must examine with
all perspicacity *how* the religious vocation must
be helped today to become aware of itself and
mature, and how religious life must "function"

in the life of the contemporary Church as a whole. To this question we are still seeking an answer—and rightly so. We can find it:

a) in the teaching of the Second Vatican Council;

b) in the exhortation *Evangelii nuntiandi;*

c) in the many statements of the Pontiffs, the Synods and the episcopal conferences.

This answer is a fundamental and multiform one. One postulate, however, seems to stand out particularly therein: if the whole life of the Church has two dimensions, the vertical and the horizontal, the religious orders must take the vertical dimension into account above all!

It is well known that the religious orders have always set great store by the vertical dimension, entering life with the Gospel and bearing witness to it with their own example. With the Gospel reread authentically: that is, on the basis of the teaching of the Church and in faithfulness to her magisterium. It must be so today also. *Testificatio—sic, contestatio—non!*

On every community, on every religious there weighs a particular co-responsibility for the real presence of Christ, who is meek and humble of heart, in the world of today—of the crucified and risen Christ—Christ among brothers: the spirit of evangelical maximalism, which is differentiated from any socio-political radicalism. "At the same time as being a challenge to the world and to the Church herself, this silent witness of poverty and abnegation, of purity and sincerity, of self-sacrifice in obedience," which religious are called to bear, "can become an eloquent witness capable of touching also non-Christians who have good will and are sensitive to certain values" (Apostolic Exhortation *Evangelii nuntiandi*, no. 69, 2).

UNITY WITH THE UNIVERSAL CHURCH

3. The joint document of the Sacred Congregation for Religious and for Secular Institutes and of the Sacred Congregation for Bishops indicates what the relationship of the orders and religious congregations must be with the episcopal college, the bishops of the individual dioceses and the episcopal conferences. It is a document of great importance, to which special attention should be devoted in the next few years, in the attempt to assume the interior attitude of maximum availability, in harmony, moreover, with that humble and ready docility which must be a distinctive note of the true religious.

Wherever you are in the world, you are, with your vocation, *"for the universal Church,"* through your mission *"in a given local Church."* Therefore, your vocation for the universal Church is realized in the structures of the local Church. Every effort must be made in order that "consecrated life" may develop in the individual local Churches, in order that it may contribute to their spiritual building up, in order that it may constitute their particular strength. Unity with the universal Church, through the local Church: that is your way.

COMMITMENT TO PRAYER

4. Before concluding, allow me to return to a point which I consider a fundamental one in the life of every religious, whatever may be the family to which he belongs. I mean the contemplative dimension, the commitment to prayer. The religious is a man consecrated to God, by means of Christ, in the charity of the Spirit. This is an ontological datum which demands to emerge to consciousness and to orientate life, not only for the benefit of the individual person, but also for the advantage of the whole community, which, in consecrated souls, experiences and enjoys in a quite special way the life-bringing presence of the divine Bridegroom.

You must not be afraid, therefore, beloved sons, to remind your confreres frequently that a pause for true worship has greater value and spiritual fruit than the most intense activity, were it apostolic activity itself. This is the most urgent "contestation" that religious must oppose to a society in which efficiency has become an idol, on the altar of which human dignity itself is not infrequently sacrificed.

Your houses must be above all centers of prayer, meditation and dialogue—personal and of the whole community—with Him who is and must remain the first and principal interlocutor in the industrious succession of your days. If you are able to nourish this "climate" of intense and loving communion with God, it will be possible for you to carry forward, without traumatic tensions or dangerous confusion, that renewal of life and discipline to which the Second Vatican Ecumenical Council committed you.

The soul that lives in habitual contact with God, and moves within the warm range of His love, can easily protect itself from the temptation of particularisms and oppositions, which create the risk of painful divisions. It can interpret in the right evangelical light the option for the poorest and for every victim of human selfishness, without surrendering to socio-political radicalizations, which in the long run turn out to be inopportune, self-defeating and often causes of new forms of tyranny. It can approach people and takes its place in the midst of the people, without questioning its own religious identity, or dimming that "specific originality" of its own vocation, which derives from the peculiar "following of Christ"—poor, chaste and obedient.

These, beloved sons, are the reflections which I was anxious to submit to your consideration in this first meeting of ours. I am certain that you will not fail to undertake to transmit them to your confreres, enriching them with the contribution of your experience and your wisdom. May you be assisted in your delicate task by the Blessed Virgin! She, whom my predecessor Paul VI of venerable memory indicated in his Apostolic Exhortation *Marialis cultus* as the Virgin listening, the Virgin in prayer, the Virgin who begets Christ and offers Him for the salvation of the world, remains the unsurpassable model of every consecrated life. May it be she who acts as your guide in the laborious but fascinating ascent towards the ideal of full assimilation with Christ the Lord.

I accompany the wish with my apostolic blessing.

Witnessing Christ by Your Lives in the Formation of the Young

On December 1, 1978, John Paul II received in audience the General Council, the Provincial Superiors and the Directors of the Italian Institutes of the Congregation of St. Joseph (Giuseppini of Murialdo), gathered in Rome for the annual organizational meeting, which coincides this time with the 150th anniversary of the birth of the Founder of the Congregation, St. Leonard Murialdo.

The Holy Father delivered an address, and the following is an excerpt.

I would like to point out a...characteristic, which seems to me important to define more completely the nature of Murialdo, and it is his deep faithfulness to the Church and to the Pope. He lived in a very difficult age for the Church, especially in Italy, and, intelligent and far-sighted as he was, he had understood perfectly that times were changing quickly and that it was better for the Church not to have any longer the concerns of "temporal power." His letters, so profound and balanced, bear witness to this. He trusted in Providence, following the example of St. Joseph, whose name your Congregation bears.

Act like this, you too! Love the Church! Love the Pope! Be docile to his teachings and his directives, convinced that the Lord wants unity in truth and in charity, and that the Holy Spirit assists the Vicar of Christ in his indispensable and salvific work. And pray, and get your young people and your faithful to pray for the Pope and for the Church.

The Role of the Seminary in the Diocesan Community

Before reciting the Angelus in St. Peter's Square on Sunday, January 14, 1979, Pope John Paul II addressed the faithful gathered there. The following is an excerpt.

The Second Vatican Council is clear and also demanding on this subject [of vocations]. One of its texts runs as follows: "The duty of fostering vocations falls on the whole Christian community, and they should discharge it principally by living full Christian lives. The greatest contribution is made by families which are animated by a spirit of faith, charity and piety and which provide, as it were, a first seminary, and by parishes in whose abundant life the young people themselves take an active part" *(Optatam totius,* no. 2).

In other words, we could say that the seminary represents an extraordinary verification of the spiritual motherhood of the Church, that is, of the People of God present in the local diocesan Church, just as individual vocations are the verification of the Christian vitality of each parish and even of individual families.

It is a question of bringing the vocation to maturity. This is possible in an atmosphere of meditation, which, however, does not exclude adequate and full preparation for "public life," that is, for that social element of the priestly ministry, characteristic of a "shepherd" who lives for his flock. It is an experience which contains a certain similarity with the hidden life at Nazareth, where our Lord "increased in wisdom and in stature, and in favor with God and man" (Lk. 2:52), preparing for His mission in the midst of the people of Israel.

Build up the Church of God in Communion

On January 23, 1979, John Paul II received in audience the members of the Permanent Council of C.E.I., meeting in Rome for its winter session. After a short address of homage delivered by Cardinal Poma, the President of C.E.I., the Holy Father delivered an address. The following is an excerpt.

...There arises the necessity of a full communion of the bishops with one another and with the successor of Peter in faith, love, aims and pastoral action.

This communion expands into the *communion of individual bishops with their own priests and men and women religious,* that is, with the souls that have given their life completely to the service of the kingdom. Here communion is expressed, on the one hand, in the concern of pastors for the spiritual and material needs of those sons who are closest to them and often most exposed to the difficulties arising from a secularized environment, and, on the other hand, in the commitment of priests and men and women religious in rallying round their bishops, listening to their voices docilely, and carrying out their directives faithfully.

COMMUNION CONSTRUCTS

Communion between bishops, clergy and religious, constructs *communion with the laity.* The latter, with all their riches of gifts and aspirations, capacity and initiatives, have a decisive task in the work of evangelizing the modern world. There may legitimately exist in the Church various degrees of connection with the hierarchical apostolate, and multiple forms of commitment in the pastoral field. From cordial acceptance of all the forces of clearly Catholic inspiration and from their utilization in plans of pastoral action, there cannot but derive an unquestionable advantage for a more and more incisive presence of the Church in the world.

It is also urgent to make an effort to restore to full ecclesial communion those movements, organisms and groups which, springing from the desire of generous and consistent adherence to the Gospel, are not yet in that community perspective which is necessary for action that is more and more aware of the joint responsibility of all the members of the People of God. It will be necessary to create new opportunities for meeting and confrontation, in an atmosphere of openness and cordiality, nourished at the table of the Word of God and the Eucharistic Bread. It will be necessary to resume dialogue patiently and trustfully, when it has been interrupted, without being discouraged by obstacles and rough patches on the way to comprehension and understanding. But that cannot be reached without obedience, due on the part of all the faithful, to the authentic magisterium of the Church, even with regard to questions connected with the doctrine concerning the faith and morality. Harmony between institutional unity and pastoral pluralism is a difficult goal, which is never reached once and for all: it depends on the unanimous and constant effort of all ecclesial members and must be sought in the light of the following axiom, which is still relevant today: *In necessariis unitas, in dubiis libertas, in omnibus caritas.* (Unity in things necessary, liberty where there is doubt, and charity in all.)

Lastly, I would like to stress that communion has its *defenses*, which, as regards bishops, can be summed up above all in prudent and courageous vigilance with regard to the insidious dangers that threaten, from outside and from within, the cohesion of the faithful round the common heritage of dogmatic truths, moral values, and disciplinary norms.

Communion has its *instruments*, first among which is your national Conference. It is right, therefore, to desire it to be more and more efficient and to be connected by an ever closer network with the other ecclesial structures, at the regional and diocesan levels.

Nor should we underestimate the instrument constituted by the press, and in particular the Catholic daily, because of the possibilities it offers of constructive dialogue among the faithful in every part of the nation, with regard to the maturing, on the personal and community plane, of choices that are responsible and, if necessary, courageously prophetic, in the context of a public opinion that is too often solicited by voices that are no longer Christian in any way. I take the liberty, therefore, of appealing to your good will, to your energies, to the organizational capacities of the individual diocese, for increasing support for such an important and meritorious cause.

TO PREACH THE GOSPEL

Since the Church is the "universal sacrament of salvation," upon her *"necessitas incumbit simulque ius sacrum evangelizandi"* (lies an obligation and at the same time a sacred right to preach the Gospel) *(Ad gentes,* no. 7).

The Lord's command to "go into all the world and preach the gospel to the whole creation" (Mk. 16:15) is the foundation of the "sacred right" of teaching her own doctrine and the moral principles which regulate human activity with regard to salvation.

Only when this "sacred right" is respected in itself and in its exercise is there put into practice that principle which the Council proclaims as the most important thing among those that regard the good of the Church, and in fact the good of the state itself, and which must always be preserved and defended everywhere, namely that "the Church in its action enjoys the freedom necessary to provide for the salvation of human beings."

This, in fact, is the sacred freedom with which God's only-begotten Son enriched the Church redeemed by His blood.

To this fundamental principle of liberty the Church appeals in her relations with the political community and, in particular, when—by common consent—she pursues the updating of the juridical instruments, ordained to healthy cooperation between Church and State, in loyal respect for the sovereignty of each, for the good of the human persons themselves.

COLLEGIAL COOPERATION

There are still many things that could be said. But in this first talk we must limit ourselves to the most important and topical ones.

I want this meeting to be the beginning of our collegial cooperation with each of you, dear and revered brothers, and with all bishops and pastors of the Church in Italy. I wish with all my heart to share your ministry, your solicitude, your difficulties, your hopes, your sufferings and your joys.

In conformity with my office, and at the same time, with full respect for the individual and collegial mission of each of you, sons of this Italian land, I would like this wish to be realized in a special way: *fecit illos Dominus crescere in plebem suam.* (The Lord made them to grow up into His own people.)

We are given new life by our common faith and the same love of Christ, who alone knows what is in man (cf. Jn. 2:25).

Let us go together to meet this man of our times—who is sometimes lost (even in this land rich in the finest Christian heritage)—by means of our service exercised in union with priests, men and women religious, and in united cooperation with all the laity.

I hope and trust that, under the protection of the Mother of the Church and the patron saints of Italy, we will be able to carry out well the mission entrusted to us by the Lord, and that our brothers and sisters will experience the joy of our communion, and will live, together with you, the great dignity of the Christian vocation.

"If You Have Met Christ, Proclaim Him!"

During the holy Mass for priests and other consecrated souls celebrated on January 26, 1979, in the Cathedral of Santo Domingo, the Holy Father delivered the following homily.

Beloved brothers and sisters,

Blessed be the Lord who has brought me here, to this soil of the Dominican Republic, where fortunately, for the glory and praise of God in this new continent, there also dawned the day of salvation. I have wished to come to this Cathedral of Santo Domingo to be for a moment in your midst, beloved priests, deacons, men and women religious, and seminarians, to manifest to you my special affection for you all, in whom the Pope and the Church put their best hopes in order that you may feel more joyful in faith, so that your pride in being what you are may overflow because of me (cf. Phil. 1:26).

Above all, however, I wish to join you in thanksgiving to God. Thanksgiving for the growth and zeal of this Church which has to its credit so many noble initiatives, and which shows such commitment in the service of God and of men. I thank God with immense joy—to use the words of the Apostle Paul—"for our partnership in the Gospel from the first day until now. And I am sure that he who began a good work in you will bring it to completion at the day of Jesus Christ" (*ibid.* 1:3ff.).

I really wish I had time to stay with you, to learn your names, and to hear from your lips "that which overflows from the heart" (cf. Mt. 12:34), the marvelous things you have experienced in your soul—*"fecit mihi magna qui potens est"* (Lk. 1:49): for He who is mighty has done great things for me—having been faithful to the meeting with the Lord. A meeting of preference on His side!

It is precisely this, the paschal meeting with the Lord, which I wish to propose to your reflection, in order to renew your faith and your enthusiasm in this Eucharistic Celebration; a personal, living meeting—with eyes wide open and a heart beating fast—with the risen Christ (cf. Lk. 24:30), the objective of your love and of your whole life.

It sometimes happens that our harmony of faith with Jesus remains weak or fades—which is at once noticed by the faithful people, who are infected with sadness by it—because, although we bear Him within us, it is sometimes in a way that is mingled with our human inclinations and reasonings (cf. *ibid.* 15), without letting all the magnificent light that He contains for us shine forth. On some occasions we may perhaps speak of Him from the standpoint of some changing premises or data of a sociological, political, psychological, linguistical character; instead of drawing the basic criteria of our life and our activity from a Gospel lived with integrity, joy, with that immense confidence and hope that the cross of Christ contains.

One thing is clear, beloved brothers: faith in the risen Christ is not the result of technical knowledge or the fruit of scientific qualifications (cf. 1 Cor. 1:26). What is asked of us is to announce the death of Jesus and to proclaim His resurrection (cf. Liturgy). Jesus is alive. "God raised him up, having loosed the bonds of death" (Acts 2:24). What was at the beginning a trembling murmur among the first witnesses, soon changed into the joyful experience of real life of those who "ate and drank with him after he rose from the dead" (Acts 10:41f.). Yes, Christ really lives in the Church; He is in us, bearers of hope and immortality.

So if you have met Christ, live Christ, live with Christ! Proclaim Him in the first person, as real witnesses: "For me to live is Christ" (Phil. 1:21). Here, too, is real liberation: to proclaim Jesus free of bonds, present in men, who are transformed, made new creatures. Why is our testimony sometimes vain? Because we present Jesus without the whole attractive power of His Person; without revealing the riches of the sublime ideal that following Him involves; because we do not always succeed in showing a conviction, expressed in real life, with regard to the stupendous value of our dedication to the great ecclesial cause that we serve.

Brothers and sisters: Men must see in us the dispensers of God's mysteries (cf. 1 Cor. 4:1), the credible witnesses of His presence in the world. Let us think frequently that God, when He calls us, does not ask for just a part of our person, but He asks us for our whole person and all our vital energies in order to proclaim to men the joy and peace of the new life in Christ, in order to guide them to the meeting with Him. Therefore, let our first care be to seek the Lord, and once we have met Him to ascertain where and how He lives, remaining with Him the whole day (Jn. 1:39). Remaining with Him, particularly in the Eucharist, where Christ gives Himself to us; and in prayer, by means of which we give ourselves to Him. The Eucharist must be completed and prolonged through prayer, in our everyday affairs as a "sacrifice of praise" (Roman Missal, Eucharistic Prayer I). In prayer, in familiar intercourse with God our Father, we discern better where our strength is and where our weakness is because the Spirit comes to our help (cf. Rom. 8:26). The same Spirit speaks to us and gradually immerses us in the divine mysteries, in the plans of love for men which God carries out by means of our offer in His service.

Like St. Paul, during a meeting at Troas to break bread, I, too, would continue to speak to you until midnight (cf. Acts 20:6ff.). I would have many more things to say but I cannot do so now. In the meantime I urge you to read carefully what I said recently in Rome, to the clergy, to men and women religious, and to seminarians. That will widen this meeting, which will continue spiritually with other similar ones in the next few days. May the Lord and our sweet Mother, the Blessed Virgin, accompany you always and fill your lives with great enthusiasm in the service of your noble ecclesial vocation.

Let us continue with Mass, placing on the table of offerings our desire to live the new life, our necessities and our supplications, the necessities and supplications of the Dominican Church and nation. Let us also put there the work and the fruits of the Third General Conference of the Latin American Episcopate at Puebla.

Dimensions of Faithfulness

During the Mass celebrated in the Cathedral of Mexico City on January 26, 1979, the Holy Father delivered the following homily.

Dear brothers in the episcopate and beloved sons,

It is only a few hours since with deep emotion I set foot for the first time on this blessed land. And now I have the happiness of this meeting with you, with the Mexican Church and people, on this *day of Mexico* as it wishes to be.

It is a meeting which began with my arrival in this beautiful city; it was extended as I passed through the streets and squares; it was intensified on my entrance into this Cathedral. But it is here, in the celebration of the Eucharistic Sacrifice, that it has its climax.

Let us put this meeting under the protection of the Mother of God, the Virgin of Guadalupe, whom the Mexican people love with the deepest devotion.

To you bishops of this Church; to you priests, men and women religious, seminarians, members of secular institutes, laity of Catholic and apostolic movements; to you children, young people, adults, and the old; to all of you Mexicans, who have a splendid past of love for Christ, even in the midst of trials; to you who bear in the depths of your heart devotion to the Virgin of Guadalupe, the Pope wishes to speak today about something which is, and must increasingly be an essential Christian and Marian feature of yours: faithfulness to the Church.

Among the many titles bestowed on the Virgin throughout the centuries by the filial love of Christians, there is one that has a very deep meaning: *Virgo Fidelis*, the faithful Virgin. What does this faithfulness of Mary's mean? What are the dimensions of this faithfulness?

The first dimension is called *search*. Mary was faithful first of all when she began, lovingly, to seek the deep sense of God's plan in her and for the world. *"Quomodo fiet?"*—How shall this be?—she asked the angel of the Annunciation. Already in the Old Testament the meaning of this search is portrayed in an expression of outstanding beauty and extraordinary spiritual content: "To seek the face of the Lord." There will not be faithfulness if it is not rooted in this ardent, patient, and generous search; if there is not in man's heart a question to which only God gives an answer, or rather, to which only God is the answer.

The second dimension of faithfulness is called *reception,* acceptance. The *"quomodo fiet?"* is changed, on Mary's lips, to *"fiat."* Let it be done, I am ready, I accept: this is the crucial moment of faithfulness, the moment in which man perceives that he will never completely understand the "how"; that there are in God's plan more areas of mystery than of clarity; that, however he may try, he will never succeed in understanding it completely. It is then that man accepts the mystery, gives it a place in his heart, just as "Mary kept all these things, pondering them in her heart" (Lk. 2:19; cf. Lk. 3:15). It is the moment when man abandons himself to the mystery, not with the resignation of one who capitulates before an enigma or an absurdity, but rather with the availability of one who opens up to be inhabited by something—by Someone!—greater than his own heart. This acceptance takes place, in short, through faith, which is the adherence of the whole being to the mystery that is revealed.

The third dimension of faithfulness is *consistency:* to live in accordance with what one believes, to adapt one's own life to the object of one's adherence. To accept misunderstandings, persecutions, rather than a break between what one practices and what one believes: this is consistency. Here is, perhaps, the deepest core of faithfulness.

But all faithfulness must pass the more exacting test: that of duration. Therefore the fourth dimension of faithfulness is *constancy.* It is easy to be consistent for a day or two. It is difficult and important to be consistent for one's whole life. It is easy to be consistent in the hour of enthusiasm; it is difficult to be so in the hour of tribulation. And only a consistency that lasts throughout the whole of life can be called faithfulness. Mary's *"fiat"* in the Annunciation finds its fullness in the silent *"fiat"* that she repeats at the foot of the cross. To be faithful means not betraying in the darkness what one has accepted in public.

Of all the teachings that the Virgin gives to her children in Mexico, the most beautiful and the most important one is perhaps this lesson of faithfulness. This faithfulness which the Pope delights in discovering and which he expects in the Mexican people.

It is said of my native country: *Polonia semper fidelis.* I want to be able to say also: Mexico *semper fidelis,* always faithful!

In fact, the religious history of this nation is a history of faithfulness; faithfulness to the seeds of faith sown by the first missionaries; faithfulness to a simple but deep-rooted religious outlook, sincere to the point of sacrifice; faithfulness to Marian devotion; exemplary faithfulness to the Pope. I did not have to come to Mexico to know this faithfulness to the Vicar of Christ, because I knew it long ago; but I thank the Lord for being able to experience it in the fervor of your welcome.

At this solemn hour I would like to call upon you to strengthen this faithfulness, to make it stauncher. I would like to call you to express it in an intelligent and strong faithfulness to the Church today. And what will be the dimensions of this faithfulness if not the same as those of Mary's faithfulness?

The Pope who visits you, expects from you a generous and noble effort to know the Church better and better. The Second Vatican Council wished to be, above all, a Council on the Church. Take in your hands the documents of the Council, especially *Lumen gentium;* study them with loving attention, with the spirit of prayer, to discover what the Spirit wished to say about the Church. In this way you will be able to realize that there is not—as some people claim—a "new

Church," different or opposed to the "old Church," but that the Council wished to reveal more clearly the one Church of Jesus Christ, with new aspects, but still the same in its essence.

The Pope expects from you, moreover, loyal acceptance of the Church. To remain attached to incidental aspects of the Church, valid in the past but outdated today, would not be faithful in this sense. Nor would it be faithful to embark, in the name of an unenlightened prophetism, on the adventurous and utopian construction of a so-called Church of the future, disembodied from the present one. We must remain faithful to the Church which, born once and for all from God's plan, from the cross, from the open sepulcher of the risen Christ and from the grace of Pentecost, is born again every day, not from the people or from other rational categories, but from the same sources as those from which it was born originally. It is born today to construct with all the nations a people desirous of growing in faith, hope and brotherly love.

Likewise the Pope expects of you that your lives should be consistent with your membership in the Church. This consistency means being aware of one's identity as a Catholic and manifesting it, with complete respect, but also without wavering or fear. The Church today needs Christians ready to bear witness clearly to their condition, and who will play their part in the mission of the Church in the world, in all social environments as a ferment of religiousness, justice, advancement of human dignity;

trying to give the world an increase of spirit so that it may be a more human and brotherly world, looking towards God.

At the same time, the Pope hopes that your consistency will not be short-lived, but constant and persevering. To belong to the Church, to live in the Church, to be the Church, is something very demanding today. Sometimes it does not cost clear and direct persecution, but it may cost contempt, indifference, underprivilege. The danger of fear, weariness, and insecurity is, therefore, easy and frequent. Do not let yourselves be overcome by these temptations. Do not allow to vanish, as a result of any of these sentiments, the strength and the spiritual energy of your "being the Church." This is a grace which we must ask for, which we must be ready to receive with great inner poverty, and which we must begin to live every morning and every day with greater fervor and intensity.

Dear brothers and sons: at this Eucharist which seals a meeting of the Servants of God with the soul and conscience of the Mexican people, the new Pope would like to gather from your lips, from your hands, and from your lives, a solemn commitment, in order to offer it to the Lord. The commitment of consecrated souls, of children, young people, adults, and the old; of cultured people and simple people, of men and women, of all: the commitment of faithfulness to Christ, to the Church of today. Let us put this intention and this commitment on the altar.

May the faithful Virgin, the Mother of Guadalupe, from whom we learn to know God's plan,

His promise and His covenant, help us with her intercession to strengthen this commitment and to carry it out until the end of our lives, until the day when the voice of the Lord will say to us: "Well done, good and faithful servant; enter into the joy of your master" (Mt. 25:21-23). Amen.

You Are Servants
of the People of God

The Holy Father delivered the following address to the priests and men religious of Mexico, who were represented in large numbers at the meeting with the Pope which took place on January 27, 1979, in the Basilica of Our Lady of Guadalupe.

Beloved priests, diocesan and religious,

One of the meetings I was most looking forward to during my visit to Mexico is that which I have with you, here in the sanctuary of our venerated and beloved Mother of Guadalupe.

See in it a proof of the Pope's affection and solicitude. He, as the Bishop of the whole Church, is aware of your irreplaceable role. He feels very close to those who are keystones in the ecclesial task, as the main collaborators of the bishops, participants in Christ's saving powers, witnesses, proclaimers of His Gospel, encouraging the faith and apostolic vocation of the People of God. And here I do not wish to forget so many other consecrated souls, precious collaborators, though without the priestly character, in many important sectors of the Church apostolate.

Not only do you have a special presence in the Church apostolate, but also your love for man through God is conspicuous among students at different levels, among the sick and those in need of assistance, among men of culture, among the poor who demand understanding and support, among so many persons who have recourse to you in search of advice and encouragement.

For your self-sacrificing dedication to the Lord and to the Church, for your closeness to man, receive my thanks in Christ's name.

Servants of a sublime cause, the fate of the Church largely depends on you in the sectors entrusted to your pastoral care. That makes it necessary for you to be deeply aware of the greatness of the mission you have received and of the necessity of better and better adapting yourselves to it.

It is a question, in fact, beloved brothers and sons, of the Church of Christ—what respect and love this must inspire in us!—which you have to serve joyfully in holiness of life (cf. Eph. 4:13).

This high and exacting service cannot be carried out without a clear and deep-rooted conviction of your identity as priests of Christ, depositaries and administrators of God's mysteries, instruments of salvation for men, witnesses of a kingdom which begins in this world but is completed in the next. In the light of these certainties of faith, why doubt about your own identity? Why hesitate about the value of your own life? Why waver on the path which you have chosen?

To preserve or strengthen this firm and persevering conviction, look at the model, Christ; renew the supernatural values in your existence; ask for strength from above, in the assiduous and trusting conversation of prayer. It is indispensable for you, today as yesterday. And also be faithful to frequent practice of the sacrament of Reconciliation, to daily meditation, to devotion to the Virgin by means of the recitation of the rosary. In a word, cultivate union with God by means of a deep inner life. Let this be your first commitment. Do not be afraid that the time dedicated to the Lord will take anything away from your apostolate. On the contrary, it will be the source of fruitfulness in the ministry.

You are persons who have made the Gospel a profession of life. You must draw from the Gospel the essential principles of faith—not mere psychological or sociological principles—which will produce a harmonious synthesis between spirituality and ministry; without permitting a "professionalization" of the latter, without diminishing the esteem that your celibacy or consecrated chastity, accepted for love of the kingdom in an unlimited spiritual fatherhood (1 Cor. 4:15), must win for you. "To them (priests) we owe our blessed regeneration"— St. John Chrysostom affirms—"and knowledge of true freedom" (*On the Priesthood*, nos. 4-6).

You are participants in Christ's ministerial priesthood for the service of the unity of the community. A service which is realized by virtue of the authority received to direct the People of God, to forgive sins and to offer the Eucharistic Sacrifice! (cf. *Lumen gentium*, no. 10; *Presbyterorum ordinis*, no. 2) A specific priestly service, which cannot be replaced in the Christian community by the common priesthood of the faithful, which is essentially different from the former! (*Lumen gentium*, no. 10)

You are members of a particular Church, whose center of unity is the bishop (*Christus Dominus,* no. 28), towards whom every priest must observe an attitude of communion and obedience. Religious, on their side, with regard to pastoral activities, cannot deny to the local hierarchy their loyal collaboration and obedience, on the pretext of exclusive dependence on the universal Church (cf. *Christus Dominus,* no. 34; *Joint Document of the Sacred Congregation for Religious and for Secular Institutes and of the Sacred Congregation for the Bishops,* May 14, 1978). Far less would it be admissible for priests or religious to practice a parallel to that of the bishops—the only authentic teachers in the faith—or of the Episcopal Conferences.

You are servants of the People of God, servants of faith, administrators and witnesses of Christ's love for men; a love that is not partisan, that excludes no one, although it is addressed preferably to the poorest. In this connection, I wish to remind you of what I said not long ago to the Superiors General of the religious in Rome: "The soul that lives in habitual contact with God, and moves within the ardent ray of His love, is able to defend itself easily against the temptation of particularisms and contrasts that create the risk of painful divisions; it is able to interpret in the correct light of the Gospel the options for the poorest and for each of the victims of human selfishness, without giving way to socio-political radicalisms which are seen in the long run to be inopportune and self-defeating" (November 24, 1978).

You are spiritual guides who endeavor to direct and improve the hearts of the faithful in order that, converted, they may live love for God and their neighbor and commit themselves to the betterment of man and to increasing his dignity.

You are priests and religious; you are not social or political leaders or officials of a temporal power. For this reason I repeat to you: "Let us not be under the illusion that we are serving the Gospel if we 'dilute' our charism through an exaggerated interest in the wide field of temporal problems" (Address to the Clergy of Rome). Let us not forget that temporal leadership can easily be a source of division, while the priest must be a sign and agent of unity and brotherhood. Secular functions are the specific field of action of laymen, who have to improve temporal matters with the Christian spirit (*Apostolicam actuositatem*, no. 4).

Beloved priests and religious: I would say many other things to you, but I do not wish to make this meeting too long. I will say some things on another occasion, and I refer you to them.

I conclude repeating to you my great confidence in you. I have great hopes in your love for Christ and for men. There is a great deal to be done. Let us set out with renewed enthusiasm, united with Christ, under the motherly gaze of the Virgin, Our Lady of Guadalupe, the sweet Mother of priests and religious. With the affectionate blessing of the Pope, for you and for all the priests and religious of Mexico.

Need of a Deep Vision of Faith

The Holy Father delivered the following address to the sisters of Mexico, represented in large numbers at the meeting with the Pope which took place in the "Miguel Angel" School, on January 27, 1979.

Beloved religious daughters of Mexico,

This meeting of the Pope with Mexican sisters, which was to have been celebrated in the Basilica of Our Mother of Guadalupe, takes place here in her spiritual presence; before her, the perfect model of woman, the best example of a life dedicated entirely to her Son the Savior, in a constant inner attitude of faith, hope, and loving dedication to a supernatural mission.

In this privileged place and before this figure of the Virgin, the Pope wishes to pass some moments with you, the many sisters present here, who represent the more than twenty thousand scattered all over Mexico and outside their homeland.

You are a very important force within the Church and within society itself, spread in innumerable sectors such as the schools and colleges, the clinics and hospitals, the field of charity and welfare, parish works, catechesis, the groups of apostolate, and so many others. You belong to different religious families, but with the same ideal within different charisms: to follow Christ, to be living witnesses to His everlasting message.

Yours is a vocation which deserves the highest esteem on the part of the Pope and the Church, yesterday as today. For this reason I wish to express to you my joyful confidence in you, and encourage you not to be discouraged along the way that you have undertaken, which is worth continuing with renewed spirit and enthusiasm. Be assured that the Pope accompanies you with his prayer, and that he delights in your faithfulness to your vocation, to Christ and to the Church.

At the same time, however, allow me to add some reflections which I propose for your consideration and examination.

It is certain that a praiseworthy spirit of faithfulness to their own ecclesial commitment prevails in a good many sisters, and that aspects of great vitality can be seen in religious life with a return to a more evangelical view, growing solidarity among religious families, greater closeness to the poor, who are given rightful priority of attention. These are reasons for joy and optimism.

But there are not lacking, either, examples of confusion with regard to the very essence of consecrated life and one's own charism. Sometimes prayer is abandoned and it is replaced by action; the vows are interpreted according to the secularizing mentality which dulls the religious motivations of one's own state; community life is abandoned with a certain irresponsibility; sociopolitical attitudes are adopted as the real aim to pursue, even with well-defined ideological radicalizations.

And when the certainties of faith are some-times dimmed, motives are put forward such as the seeking of new horizons and experiences, perhaps with the pretext of being closer to men, maybe concrete groups, chosen with criteria that are not always evangelical.

Beloved sisters: never forget that to maintain a clear concept of the value of your consecrated life you need a deep vision of faith, which is nourished and preserved with prayer (cf. *Perfectae caritatis*, no. 6). This faith will enable you to overcome all uncertainty with regard to your own identity, and will keep you faithful to that vertical dimension which is essential for you in order to identify you with Christ from the beatitudes, and in order to be true witnesses to the kingdom of God for men of the modern world.

Only with this concern for the interests of Christ (cf. 1 Cor. 7:32) will you be capable of giving to the charism of prophecy its suitable dimension of witness to the Lord: without options for the poor and needy which do not spring from the criteria of the Gospel, but are inspired by socio-political motivations which—as I said recently to the Mother Superiors General in Rome—turn out in the long run to be inopportune and self-defeating.

You have chosen as a way of life the pursuit of some values which are not merely human ones, although you must also esteem the latter in their rightful measure. You have opted for service of others for love of God. Never forget that the human being is not exhausted in the earthly dimension only. You, as professionals of faith and experts in the sublime knowledge of Christ (cf. Phil. 3:8), open them to the call and dimension of eternity in which you yourselves must live.

I would have many other things to tell you. Take as said to you what I indicated to the Mother Superiors General in my address of last November 16. How much you can do today for the Church and for mankind! They are waiting for your generous commitment, the dedication of your free heart, expanding in an unsuspected way its potentialities of love in a world that is losing the capacity of altruism, self-sacrificing and disinterested love. Remember, in fact, that you are mystical brides of Christ and of Christ crucified (cf. 2 Cor. 4:5).

The Church repeats to you today her trust: be living witnesses to this new civilization of love, which my predecessor Paul VI rightly proclaimed.

In order that strength from above may support you in this magnificent and hopeful enterprise, that it will keep you, in renewed spiritual youth, faithful to these resolutions, I accompany you with a special blessing, which I extend to all the sisters of Mexico.

Our Pastoral Service Compels Us To Preserve, Defend, and Communicate the Truth

On January 28, 1979, in the Major Seminary Palafoxiano of Puebla de Los Angeles, there opened the Third General Conference of the Latin-American Episcopate. Before the representatives of all the bishops of Latin America Pope John Paul II delivered a discourse. The following is an excerpt.

Unity with priests, religious and faithful:

Let unity among the bishops be extended by unity with priests, religious and faithful. Priests are the immediate collaborators of the bishops in their pastoral mission, and their mission would be compromised if close unity did not reign between priests and bishops.

Men and women religious are also especially important subjects of that unity. I well know the importance of their contribution to evangelization in Latin America in the past and in the present. They came here at the dawn of the discovery and accompanied the first steps of almost all the countries. They worked continuously here together with the diocesan clergy. In some countries more than half, in other countries the great majority, of the body of priests are religious. This would be enough to show how important it is here more than in other parts of the world for religious not only to accept but to seek loyally an unbreakable unity of aim and action with their bishops. To the bishops the Lord entrusted the mission of feeding the flock. To religious it belongs to blaze the trails for evangelization. It cannot be, it ought not to be, that the bishops should lack the responsible and active, yet at the same time, docile and trusting collaboration of the religious, whose charism makes them ever more ready agents at the service of the Gospel. In this matter everybody in the ecclesial community has the duty of avoiding magisteria other than the Church's magisterium, for they are ecclesially unacceptable and pastorally sterile.

The laity also are subjects of that unity, whether involved individually or joined in apostolic associations for the spreading of the kingdom of God. It is they who have to consecrate the world to Christ in the midst of their daily duties and in their various family and professional tasks, in close union with and obedience to the lawful pastors.

In line with *Lumen gentium*, we must safeguard the precious gift of ecclesial unity between all those who form part of the pilgrim People of God.

DEFENDERS AND PROMOTERS OF HUMAN DIGNITY

Those familiar with the Church's history know that in all periods there have been admirable bishops deeply involved in advancing and valiantly defending the human dignity of those entrusted to them by the Lord. They have always been impelled to do so by their episcopal mission, because they considered human dignity a Gospel value that cannot be despised without greatly offending the Creator.

This dignity is infringed on the individual level when due regard is not had for values such as freedom, the right to profess one's religion, physical and mental integrity, the right to essential goods, to life.... It is infringed on the social and political level when man cannot exercise his right of participation, of when he is subjected to unjust and unlawful coercion, or submitted to physical or mental torture, etc.

I am not unaware of how many questions are being posed in this sphere today in Latin America. As bishops, you cannot fail to concern yourselves with them. I know that you propose to carry out a serious reflection on the relationships and implications between evangelization and human advancement or liberation, taking into consideration, in such a vast and important field, what is specific about the Church's presence.

Here is where we find, brought concretely into practice, the themes we have touched upon in speaking of the truth concerning Christ, the Church and man.

If the Church makes herself present in the defense of, or in the advancement of, man, she does so in line with her mission, which, although it is religious and not social or political, cannot fail to consider man in the entirety of his being. The Lord outlined in the parable of the Good Samaritan the model of attention to all human needs (cf. Lk. 10:29ff.), and He said that in the final analysis He will identify Himself with the disinherited—the sick, the imprisoned, the hungry, the lonely—who have been given a helping hand (Mt. 25:31ff.). The Church has learned in these and other pages of the Gospel (cf. Mk. 6:35-44) that her evangelizing mission has, as an essential part, action for justice and the tasks of the advancement of man (cf. final document of the Synod of Bishops, October 1971), and that between evangelization and human advancement there are very strong links of the orders of anthropology, theology and love (cf. *Evangelii nuntiandi*, no. 31); so that "evangelization would not be complete if it did not take into account the unceasing interplay of the Gospel and of man's concrete life, both personal and social" *(Evangelii nuntiandi, no. 29)*.

Let us also keep in mind that the Church's action in earthly matters such as human advancement, development, justice, the rights of the individual, is always intended to be at the service of man; and of man as she sees him in the Christian vision of the anthropology that she adopts. She therefore does not need to have recourse to ideological systems in order to love, defend and collaborate in the liberation of man: at the center of the message of which she is the depositary and herald she finds inspiration for acting in favor of brotherhood, justice, and peace, against all forms of domination, slavery, discrimination, violence, attacks on religious liberty and aggression against man, and whatever attacks life (cf. *Gaudium et spes,* nos. 26, 27 and 29).

It is therefore not through opportunism nor thirst for novelty that the Church, "the expert in humanity" (Paul VI, Address to the United Nations, October 4, 1965) defends human rights. It is through a true *evangelical commitment,* which, as happened with Christ, is a commitment to the most needy. In fidelity to this commitment, the Church wishes to stay free with regard to the competing systems, in order to opt only for man. Whatever the miseries or sufferings that afflict man, it is not through violence, the interplay of power and political systems, but through the truth concerning man, that he journeys towards a better future.

Hence the Church's constant preoccupation with the delicate question of property. A proof of this is the writings of the Fathers of the Church through the first thousand years of Christianity (cf. St. Ambrose, *De Nabuthe,* c. 12, no. 52; *PL* 14, 747). It is clearly shown by the vigorous teaching of St. Thomas Aquinas, repeated so many times. In our own times, the Church has appealed to the same principles in such far-reaching documents as the social encyclicals of the recent Popes. With special force and profundity, Pope Paul VI spoke of this subject in his encyclical *Populorum progressio* (cf. nos. 23-24; cf. also *Mater et magistra,* 1.06).

This voice of the Church, echoing the voice of human conscience, and which did not cease to make itself heard down the centuries in the midst of the most varied social and cultural systems and conditions, deserves and needs to be heard in our time also, when the growing wealth of a few parallels the growing poverty of the masses.

It is then that the Church's teaching, according to which all private property involves a social obligation, acquires an urgent character. With respect to this teaching, the Church has a mission to carry out; she must preach, educate individuals and collectivities, form public opinion, and offer orientations to the leaders of the peoples. In this way she will be working in favor of society, within which this Christian and evangelical principle will finally bear the fruit of a more just and equitable distribution of goods, not only within each nation but also in the world in general, ensuring that the stronger countries do not use their power to the detriment of the weaker ones.

Those who bear responsibility for the public life of the states and nations will have to understand that internal peace and international peace can only be ensured if a social and economic system based on justice flourishes.

Christ did not remain indifferent in the face of this vast and demanding imperative of social morality. Nor could the Church. In the spirit of the Church, which is the spirit of Christ, and relying upon her ample and solid doctrine, let us return to work in this field.

It must be emphasized here once more that the Church's solicitude looks to the whole man.

For this reason, for an economic system to be just it is an indispensable condition that it should favor the development and diffusion of public education and culture. The more just the economy, the deeper will be the conscience of culture. This is very much in line with what the Council stated: that to attain a life worthy of man, it is not possible to limit oneself to *having more;* one must aspire to *being more* (cf. *Gaudium et spes,* no. 35).

Therefore, brothers, drink at these authentic fountains. Speak with the language of the Council, of John XXIII, of Paul VI: it is the language of the experience, of the suffering, of the hope of modern humanity.

When Paul VI declared that development is "the new name of peace" (*Populorum progressio,* no. 76), he had in mind all the links of interdependence that exist not only within the nations but also those outside them, on the world level. He took into consideration the mechanisms that, because they happen to be imbued not with authentic humanism but with materialism, produce on the international level rich people ever more rich at the expense of poor people ever more poor.

There is no economic rule capable of changing these mechanisms by itself. It is necessary, in international life, to call upon ethical principles, the demands of justice, the primary commandment which is that of love. Primacy must be given to what is moral, to what is spiritual, to what springs from the full truth concerning man.

I have wished to manifest to you these reflections which I consider very important, although they must not distract you from the central theme of the conference: we shall reach man, we shall reach justice, through evangelization.

In the face of what has been said hitherto, the Church sees with deep sorrow "the sometimes massive increase of human rights violations in all parts of society and of the world.... Who can deny that today individual persons and civil powers violate basic rights of the human person with impunity: rights such as the right to be born, the right to life, the right to responsible pro-creation, to work, to peace, to freedom and social justice, the right to participate in the decisions that affect people and nations? And what can be said when we face the various forms of collective violence like discrimination against individuals and groups, the use of physical and psychological torture perpetrated against prisoners or political dissenters? The list grows when we turn to the instance of the abduction of persons for political reasons and look at the acts of kidnapping for material gain which attack so dramatically family life and the social fabric" (Message of John Paul II to the Secretary-General of the United Nations Organization on December 2, 1978: 30th Anniversary of the Declaration of Human Rights). We cry out once more: Respect man! He is the image of God! Evangelize, so that this may become a reality: so that the Lord may transform hearts and humanize the political and economic systems, with man's responsible commitment as the starting point!

Pastoral commitments in this field must be encouraged through a correct Christian idea of liberation. The Church feels the duty to proclaim the liberation of millions of human beings, the duty to help this liberation become firmly established (cf. *Evangelii nuntiandi*, no. 30); but she also feels the corresponding duty to proclaim liberation in its integral and profound meaning, as Jesus proclaimed and realized it (cf. *Evangelii nuntiandi*, no. 31). "Liberation from everything that oppresses man but which is, above all, liberation from sin and the evil one, in the joy of knowing God and being known by Him" *(Evangelii nuntiandi*, no. 9). Liberation made up of reconciliation and forgiveness. Liberation springing from the reality of being children of God, whom we are able to call Abba, Father (Rom. 8:15); a reality which makes us recognize in every man a brother of ours, capable of being transformed in his heart through God's mercy. Liberation that, with the energy of love, urges us towards fellowship, the summit and fullness of which we find in the Lord. Liberation as the overcoming of the various forms of slavery and man-made idols, and as the growth of the new man. Liberation that in the framework of the Church's proper mission is not reduced to the simple and narrow economic, political, social or cultural dimension, and is not sacrificed to the demands of any strategy, practice or short-term solution (cf. *Evangelii nuntiandi*, no. 33).

To safeguard the originality of Christian liberation and the energies that it is capable of releasing, one must at all costs avoid any form of curtailment or ambiguity, as Pope Paul VI asked: "The Church would lose her fundamental meaning. Her message of liberation would no longer have any originality and would easily be open to monopolization and manipulation by ideological

systems and political parties" *(Evangelii nuntiandi,* no. 32). There are many signs that help to
distinguish when the liberation in question is
Christian and when on the other hand it is based
rather on ideologies that rob it of consistency
with an evangelical view of man, of things and of
events (cf. *Evangelii nuntiandi,* no. 35). They are
signs drawn from the content of what the evangelizers proclaim or from the concrete attitudes
that they adopt. At the level of content, one must
see what is their fidelity to the word of God, to the
Church's living Tradition and to her magisterium. As for attitudes, one must consider what
sense of communion they have with the bishops,
in the first place, and with the other sectors of the
People of God; what contribution they make to
the real building up of the community; in what
form they lovingly show care for the poor, the
sick, the dispossessed, the neglected and the oppressed, and in what way they find in them the
image of the poor and suffering Jesus, and strive
to relieve their need and serve Christ in them (cf.
Lumen gentium, no. 8). Let us not deceive ourselves: the humble and simple faithful, as though
by an evangelical instinct, spontaneously sense
when the Gospel is served in the Church and
when it is emptied of its content and is stifled
with other interests.

As you see, the series of observations made
by *Evangelii nuntiandi* on the theme of liberation retains all its validity.

What we have already recalled constitutes
a rich and complex heritage, which *Evangelii
nuntiandi* calls the Social Doctrine or Social

Teaching of the Church (cf. *Evangelii nuntiandi*, no. 38). This teaching comes into being, in the light of the Word of God and the authentic magisterium, from the presence of Christians in the midst of the changing situations of the world, in contact with the challenges that result from those situations. This social doctrine involves therefore both principles for reflection and also norms for judgment and guidelines for action (cf. *Octogesima adveniens*, no. 4).

Placing responsible confidence in this social doctrine—even though some people seek to sow doubts and lack of confidence in it—to give it serious study, to try to apply it, to teach it, to be faithful to it: all this is the guarantee, in a member of the Church, of his commitment in the delicate and demanding social tasks, and of his efforts in favor of the liberation or advancement of his brothers and sisters.

Allow me therefore to recommend to your special pastoral attention the urgent need to make your faithful people aware of this social doctrine of the Church.

Particular care must be given to forming a social conscience at all levels and in all sectors. When injustices grow worse and the distance between rich and poor increases distressingly, the social doctrine, in a form which is creative and open to the broad fields of the Church's presence, must be a valuable instrument for formation and action. This holds good particularly for the laity: "It is to the laity, though not exclusively to them, that secular duties and activity properly belong" (*Gaudium et spes*, no. 43). It is necessary to avoid supplanting the laity and to study seriously just when certain forms of supplying for them retain their reason for existence. Is it not the laity who are called, by reason of their vocation in the Church, to make their contribution in the political and economic dimensions, and to be effectively present in the safeguarding and advancement of human rights?

SOME PRIORITY TASKS

You are going to consider many pastoral themes of great significance. Time prevents me from mentioning them. Some I have referred to or will do so in the meetings with the priests, religious, seminarians and lay people.

The themes that I indicate here have, for different reasons, great importance. You will not fail to consider them, among the many others that your pastoral farsightedness will indicate to you.

a) The Family: Make every effort to ensure that there is pastoral care for the family. Attend to this field of such primary importance in the certainty that evangelization in the future depends largely on the "domestic Church." It is the school of love, of the knowledge of God, of respect for life and for human dignity. The importance of this pastoral care is in proportion to the threats aimed at the family. Think of the campaigns in favor of divorce, of the use of contraceptive practices, and of abortion, which destroy society.

St. Andrew Convent

b) Priestly and religious vocations: In the majority of your countries, in spite of an encouraging awakening of vocations, the lack of vocations is a grave and chronic problem. There is a huge disproportion between the growing population and the number of agents of evangelization. This is of great importance to the Christian community. Every community has to obtain its vocations, as a sign of its vitality and maturity. Intense pastoral activity must be reactivated, starting with the Christian vocation in general and from enthusiastic pastoral care for youth, so as to give the Church the ministers she needs. Lay vocations, although they are so indispensable, cannot compensate for them. Furthermore, one of the proofs of the laity's commitment is an abundance of vocations to the consecrated life.

c) Youth: How much hope the Church places in youth! How much energy needed by the Church abounds in youth in Latin America! How close we pastors must be to the young, so that Christ and the Church and love of the brethren may penetrate deeply into their hearts.

CONCLUSION

At the end of this message I cannot fail to invoke once again the protection of the Mother of God upon your persons and your work during these days. The fact that this meeting of ours is taking place in the spiritual presence of Our Lady of Guadalupe, who is venerated in Mexico and in all the other countries as the Mother of the Church in Latin America, is for me a cause for joy and a source of hope. May she, the "Star of evangelization," be your guide in your future reflections and decisions. May she obtain for you from her divine Son:

—the boldness of prophets and the evangelical prudence of pastors,

—the clearsightedness of teachers and the reliability of guides and directors,

—courage as witnesses, and the calmness, patience and gentleness of fathers.

May the Lord bless your labors. You are accompanied by select representatives: priests, deacons, men and women religious, lay people, experts and observers, whose collaboration will be very useful to you. The whole Church has its eyes on you, with confidence and hope. You intend to respond to these expectations with full fidelity to Christ, the Church, and humanity. The future is in God's hands, but in a certain way God places that future with new evangelizing momentum in your hands, too. "Go therefore and make disciples of all nations" (Mt. 28:19).

Consecrated Life Is Relevant Today

On January 30, 1979, on his way from the "Santa Cecilia" district to the Basilica of Our Lady of Zapopán, Pope John Paul II made a short stop at Guadalajara Cathedral, where many enclosed nuns were waiting for him. The Holy Father delivered the following address.

Beloved enclosed sisters,

In this Cathedral of Guadalajara, I wish to greet you with the beautiful and expressive words that we frequently repeat in the liturgical assembly: "May the Lord be with you" (Roman Missal). Yes, may the Lord, to whom you have dedicated your whole life, always be with you.

How could a meeting of the Pope with contemplative sisters fail to take place during the visit to Mexico? If I would like to see so many persons, you have a special place because of your particular consecration to the Lord and to the Church. For this reason, the Pope, too, wishes to be close to you.

This meeting wishes to be the continuation of the one I had with other Mexican sisters. I said many things to them which are also for you, but now I wish to refer to what is more specifically yours.

How often the magisterium of the Church has shown its great esteem for, and appreciation of, your life dedicated to prayer, silence and to an exceptional way of dedication to God! In these moments when everything is changing so much, does this type of life continue to have a meaning or is it something that is already outdated?

The Pope tells you: Yes, your life is more important than ever, your complete consecration is fully relevant today. In a world that is losing the sense of the divine, in the light of the over-estimation of material things, you, beloved sisters, committed from your cloisters to be witnesses of certain values for which you live, be witnesses to the Lord for the world of today, and instill with your prayer a new breath of life into the Church and into modern man.

Especially in contemplative life, it is a question of realizing a difficult unity: to manifest to the world the mystery of the Church in this world and to enjoy here already, teaching them to men, as St. Paul says, "the things that are above" (Col. 3:1).

Being a contemplative does not mean breaking radically with the world, with the apostolate. The contemplative has to find her specific way of extending the kingdom of God, of collaborating in the building up of the earthly city, not only with her prayers and sacrifices, but also with her testimony, silent, it is true, yet which can be understood by the men of good will with whom she is in contact.

For this reason you have to find your own style which, within a contemplative vision, will let you share with your brothers the gratuitous gift of God.

Your consecrated life comes from baptismal consecration and expresses it with greater fullness. With a free response to the call of the

Holy Spirit, you decided to follow Christ, consecrating yourselves to Him completely. "The more stable and firm this bond (the unbreakable bond of union that exists between Christ and His Church) is,"—the Council says—"the more perfect will the Christian's religious consecration be" (*Lumen gentium*, no. 4).

You contemplative religious women feel an attraction that brings you to the Lord. Relying on God, you abandon yourselves to His fatherly action which raises you to Him and transforms you into Him, while He prepares you for eternal contemplation which is the ultimate goal for us all. How could you advance along this path and be faithful to the grace that animates you, if you did not respond with your whole being, by means of a dynamism the impulse of which is love, to this call that directs you permanently to God? So, consider any other activity as a testimony, offered to the Lord, of your deep communion with Him, so that He may grant you that purity of intention which is so necessary in order to meet Him in prayer itself. In this way you will contribute to the extension of the kingdom of God, with the testimony of your life and with a "hidden apostolic fruitfulness" (*Perfectae caritatis*, no. 7).

Gathered in Christ's name, your communities have as their center the Eucharist, "a sacrament of love, a sign of unity, a bond of charity" (*Sacrosanctum concilium*, no. 47).

Through the Eucharist, the world also is present at the center of your life of prayer and offering, as the Council explained: "Let no one think that their consecrated way of life alienates religious from other men or makes them useless for human society. Though in some cases they have no direct relations with their contemporaries, still in a deeper way they have their fellow men present with them in the heart of Christ and cooperate with them spiritually, so that the building up of human society may always have its foundation in the Lord and have Him as its goal: otherwise those who build it may have labored in vain" *(Lumen gentium,* no. 46).

Contemplating you with the tenderness of the Lord when He called His disciples "little flock" (cf. Lk. 12:32) and announced to them that His Father had been pleased to give them the kingdom, I beg you: keep the simplicity of the "little ones" of the Gospel. Know how to find it in intimate and deep relations with Christ and in contact with your brothers. You will then know "overflowing joy through the action of the Holy Spirit," the joy of those who are introduced into the secrets of the kingdom (cf. *Apostolic Exhortation on the Renewal of Religious Life,* no. 54).

May the beloved Mother of the Lord, whom you invoke in Mexico with the sweet name of Our Lady of Guadalupe, and following whose example you have dedicated your life to God, obtain for you, on your daily path, that unfailing joy that only Jesus can give.

Receive my warm apostolic blessing as a great greeting of peace which is not exhausted in you present here, but which extends invisibly to all your contemplative sisters in Mexico.

Dedicate Yourself to Christ and Devote Yourself to Man in Christ

After Mass in Zapopán Basilica, on January 30, 1979, John Paul II went to visit the Major Seminary of Guadalajara where the major seminarians—diocesan and religious—of the whole of Mexico were waiting for him. The Pope delivered the following address.

Dear seminarians, diocesan and religious, of Mexico,

May the peace of the Lord be with you always!

The exuberant and affectionate enthusiasm with which you have received me this afternoon moves me deeply. I feel an immense joy on sharing with you these moments which confirm beyond any doubt, on your side, the appreciation you feel before God for the Pope; and this instills in me consolation and new courage (cf. 2 Cor. 7:13).

Through you, my inner joy extends to my dear brothers in the episcopate, to priests, religious and to all the faithful. Let my deepest gratitude go to all for so many attentions and for such filial cordiality, and even more for remembering me in their prayers to the Lord. I can assure you that your unanimous response to this "pastoral visit" of mine to Mexico has given form in me, during these days, to a welcome presentiment. I will express it in the words of the Apostle: "I rejoice, because I have perfect confidence in you" (2 Cor. 7:16).

1. It is a motive of satisfaction for me to know that Mexican seminaries have a long and glorious tradition which goes back to the times of the Council of Trent, with the foundation of the college "San Pedro" in this city of Guadalajara, in 1570. In the course of time, many other centers of priestly formation, scattered all over the national territory, were added to this one, as a persistent proof of a fresh and vigorous ecclesial vitality. I do not want to pass over in silence the already centenarian Mexican College in Rome. It has a very important mission: to keep alive the bond between Mexico and the Pope's Chair. I consider it the indispensable duty of all to help it and sustain it, so that it can carry out this fundamental task in full faithfulness to the norms of the magisterium and to the guidelines given by Peter's See.

This historical concern to create new seminaries arouses in me feelings of satisfaction and approval; but what particularly fills me with hope is the continual flourishing of priestly and religious vocations. I feel happy to see you here, young people overflowing with joy, because you have answered "yes" to the Lord's invitation to serve Him, body and soul, in the Church, in the ministerial priesthood. Like St. Paul, I wish to throw my heart wide open to you, to say to you: "Our heart is wide.... In return...widen your hearts also" (2 Cor. 6:11-13).

2. Just over two months ago, when I had just begun my pontificate, I had a *eucharistic audience* with the seminarians of Rome. As I did then, today I invite you, too, to listen carefully to the Lord who speaks to the heart, especially in prayer and in the liturgy, to discover and to root in the depths of your being the meaning and the value of your vocation.

God, who is truth and love, manifested Himself to us in the history of creation and in the history of salvation: a history that is still incomplete, that of mankind, which "waits with eager longing for the revealing of the sons of God" (cf. Rom. 8:18f.). The same God chose us, called us to instill new strength into this history, already knowing that salvation "is the gift of God, [coming] not because of works, we are His workmanship, created in Christ Jesus" (Eph. 2:8-10). A history, therefore, which is in God's plans, and is also ours, because God wishes us to be workers in the vineyard (cf. Mt. 20:1-16); He wants us to be ambassadors to go and meet everyone and invite everyone to His banquet (*ibid.* 22:1-14); He wants us to be Good Samaritans who have pity on our unfortunate neighbor (Lk. 10:30ff.).

3. This would already be enough to see from closer up how great is the vocation. To experience it is a unique event, inexpressible, perceived only as a sweet breath through the awakening touch of grace: a breath of the Spirit who, while He gives a real form to our frail human reality—a clay vessel in the hands of the

potter (Rom. 9:20-21)—also lights in our hearts a new light, instills an extraordinary strength which, consolidating us in love, incorporates our existence with the work of God, with His plan of *re-creating* man in Christ, that is, the formation of His new redeemed family. You are, therefore, called to construct the Church—communion with God—something far above what one can ask or imagine (cf. Eph. 3:14-21).

4. Dear seminarians, who one day will be ministers of God to plant and water the Lord's field, take advantage of these years in the seminary to fill yourselves with the feeling of Christ Himself, in study, prayer, obedience, and the formation of your character. In this way, you will yourselves see how, in proportion as your vocation matures in this school, your life will joyfully assume a specific character, a precise indication: the orientation towards others, like Christ, who "went about doing good and healing all" (Acts 10:38). In this way, what might seem a misfortune on the human plane is transformed into a luminous project of life, already examined and approved by Jesus: to live not to be served but to serve (Mt. 20:28).

As you well understand, nothing is further from the vocation than the incentive of earthly advantages, than pursuit of benefits or honors; and the vocation is also very far from being escape from an environment of frustrated hopes or from one which is hostile or alienating. The good news, for him who is called to service of the People of God, in addition to being a call to change and improve one's own existence, is also a call to a life already transformed in Christ, who must be proclaimed and spread.

Let that suffice, dear seminarians. You will be able to add the rest yourselves, with your open and generous hearts. I want to add just one thing: love your directors, educators, and superiors. On them there falls the agreeable but difficult task of leading you by the hand along the way that goes to the priesthood. They will help you to acquire a taste for interior life, for the demanding habit of renunciation for Christ, and for disinterestedness; above all, they will infect you with "the fragrance of the knowledge of Christ" (cf. 2 Cor. 2:14). Do not be afraid. The Lord is with you, and at every moment He is our best guarantee: "I know whom I have believed" (2 Tm. 1:12).

With this trust in the Lord, open your hearts to the action of the Holy Spirit; open them in a resolution of dedication that knows no reservations; open them to the world which is expecting you and needs you; open them to the call already addressed to you by so many souls, to whom, one day, you will be able to give Christ, in the Eucharist, in Penance, in the preaching of the revealed Word, in friendly and disinterested advice, in the serene testimony of your lives as men who are in the world without being of the world.

It is worth dedicating oneself to the cause of Christ, who wants valiant and decided hearts; it is worth devoting oneself to man for Christ, in order to bring him to Him, to raise him, to help him on his way to eternity; it is worth making an option for an ideal that will give you great joys, even if at the same time it demands a good many sacrifices. The Lord does not abandon His followers.

For the kingdom, it is worth living this precious value of Christianity, priestly celibacy, the centuries-old heritage of the Church; it is worth living it in a responsible way, although it calls for a good many sacrifices. Cultivate devotion to Mary, the Virgin Mother of the Son of God, so that she may help you and urge you to carry it out fully!

But I would also like to reserve a special word for you, educators and superiors of houses of formation to the priesthood. You have a treasure of the Church in your hands. Look after it with the greatest attention and diligence, so that it may produce the hoped-for fruits. Form these young men to wholesome joy, cultivating a rich personality adapted to our time. But form this personality staunch in the faith, in the principles of the Gospel, in awareness of the value of souls, in the spirit of prayer, capable of facing up to the onslaughts of the future.

Do not shorten the vertical view of life, do not lower the exigencies that the option for Christ imposes. If we propose ideals that are distorted, the young will be the first not to want them, because they desire something that is worthwhile, an ideal that is worthy of an existence: although there is a price to pay.

You who are responsible for vocations, priests, religious, fathers and mothers of families, I address these words to you. Commit yourselves generously to the task of procuring new vocations, so important for the future of the Church. The shortage of vocations call for a responsible effort to remedy it. And this will not be obtained if we are not able to pray, if we are not able to give the vocation to the diocesan or religious priesthood the appreciation and the esteem it deserves.

Young seminarians! I give all of you my blessing. Christ is waiting for you. You cannot disappoint Him.

Christ Illumines the Mystery of Man

On February 2, 1979, the feast of the Presentation of the Lord, Pope John Paul II celebrated holy Mass in St. Peter's Basilica for men and women religious. In the course of the ceremonies he blessed the candles, symbols of the light that Christ gave to the world with His coming.

The Holy Father delivered the following homily.

1. *Lumen ad revelationem gentium* (a light for revelation to the gentiles.)

The liturgy of today's feast recalls, in the first place, the words of the prophet Malachi: "the Lord whom you seek will suddenly come to his temple...behold, he is coming." These words, in fact, come true at this moment: there enters His temple for the first time He who is its Lord. It is a question of the temple of the Old Covenant, which was the preparation for the New Covenant. God makes this New Covenant with His people in Him whom "he anointed and sent into the world," that is, in His Son. The temple of the Old Covenant waits for that Anointed One, the Messiah. The reason for its existence, so to speak, is this waiting.

And here He enters, brought by the hands of Mary and Joseph. He enters as an infant, forty days old, in order to meet the requirement of Mosaic law. He is brought to the temple like so many other Israelite children: the child of poor parents. So He enters unobserved and—almost in contrast with the words of the prophet Malachi

—not expected by anyone. *Deus absconditus* (the hidden God; cf. Is. 45:15). Hidden in human flesh, born in a stable near the town of Bethlehem. Subject to the law of redemption, as His Mother was to the law of purification.

Although everything seems to indicate that here, at this moment, no one is expecting Him and no one notices Him, actually it is not so. The aged Simeon goes up to Mary and Joseph, takes the child in his arms, and utters the words that are a living echo of the prophecy of Isaiah:

"Lord, now let your servant depart in peace, according to your word; for mine eyes have seen your salvation which you have prepared in the presence of all peoples, a light for revelation to the Gentiles, and for glory to your people Israel" (Lk. 2:29-32).

These words are a synthesis of the whole expectation, a synthesis of the Old Covenant. The man who utters them does not speak by himself. He is a prophet: he speaks from the depth of the Revelation and of the faith of Israel. He announces the fulfillment of the Old and the beginning of the New.

CANDLES SYMBOLIZE
CHRIST THE LORD

2. The light.

Today the Church blesses the candles which give light. These candles are, at the same time, a symbol of the other light, the light that is Christ. He began to be Light from the moment of His birth. He was revealed as Light to the eyes of Simeon on the fortieth day after His birth. Then He remained as Light for thirty years in the hidden life of Nazareth. Subsequently, He began to teach, and the period of His teaching was a short one. He said: "I am the light of the world; he who follows me will not walk in darkness, but will have the light of life" (Jn. 8:12). When He was crucified "there was darkness over all the land" (Mt. 27:45 and sim.), but on the third day this darkness made way for the light of the resurrection.

The Light is with us!

What does it illumine?

It illumines the darkness of human souls. The darkness of existence. Man makes a perennial and immense effort to open up a way and arrive at light; the light of knowledge and existence. How many years does not man at times dedicate to clarifying some fact for himself, to finding the answer to a given question! And how much personal toil it costs each of us in order that—through everything in us that is "dark," shadowy, through our "worse self," through the man subjugated by the lust of the flesh, the lust of the eyes, and the pride of life (cf. 1 Jn. 2:16) —we can reveal what is luminous: the man of simplicity, of humility, of love, of disinterested sacrifice; the new horizons of thought, of the heart, of will, of character. "The darkness is passing away and the true light is already shining," St. John writes (1 Jn. 2:8).

If we ask what is illuminated by this light, recognized by Simeon in the Child forty days old, the answer is as follows: it is the answer of the interior experience of so many men who have decided to follow this light. It is the answer of your life, my dear brothers and sisters, men and women religious who take part today in the liturgy of this feast, holding a lighted candle in your hands. It is, as it were, a foretaste of the paschal vigil when the Church, that is each of us, holding high the lighted candle, will cross the threshold of the temple, singing *Lumen Christi*. It is particularly in depth that Christ illumines the mystery of man. Particularly and deeply, and with what delicacy, He descends into the secret recesses of souls and of human consciences. He is the Master of life, in the deepest sense. Yet just He, He, the only one, has revealed to each of us, and always reveals to so many men, the truth that "man, who is the only creature on earth which God willed for itself, cannot fully find himself except through a sincere gift of himself (cf. Lk. 17:33)" (Pastoral Constitution *Gaudium et spes*, no. 24).

Let us give thanks today for the light that is in the midst of us. Let us give thanks for everything that, by means of Christ, has become light in ourselves, has ceased to be "darkness and the unknown."

LIGHT ILLUMINES THE DARKNESS

3. Finally, Simeon says to Mary, first with regard to her Son: "Behold, this child is set for the fall and rising of many in Israel, and for a sign

that is spoken against." Then with regard to herself: "And a sword will pierce through your own soul also, that thoughts out of many hearts may be revealed" (Lk. 2:34-35).

This day is His feast: the feast of Jesus Christ, on the fortieth day of His life, in the temple of Jerusalem according to the provisions of the law of Moses (cf. Lk. 2:22-24). And it is also her feast: Mary's.

She carries the Child in her arms. He, even in her hands, is the Light of our souls, the Light that illumines the darkness of knowledge and of human existence, of the intellect and the heart.

The thoughts of so many hearts are revealed when her mother's hands carry this great divine Light, when they bring it closer to man.

Hail, you who became Mother of our Light at the cost of the great sacrifice of your Son, at the cost of the motherly sacrifice of your heart!

4. And, finally, allow me, today, on the day after my return from Mexico, to thank you, O Lady of Guadalupe, for this Light which your Son is for the sons and daughters of that country and also of the whole of Latin America. The Third General Conference of the Episcopate of that continent, which began solemnly at your feet, O Mary, in the Sanctuary of Guadalupe, has been carrying out its work in Puebla since January 28 on the subject of the evangelization of Latin America in the present and in the future. It is endeavoring to show the ways along which the light of Christ must reach

the contemporary generation in that great and promising continent.

Let us recommend this work in prayer, looking today at Christ carried in His Mother's arms, and listening to Simeon's words: *Lumen ad revelationem gentium.*

Holy Father Urges Church
To Continue Prayers
for Aims of Latin America

On February 14, 1979, at the general audience in Paul VI Hall, Pope John Paul addressed those present. An excerpt follows:

The future of evangelization is identified with the implementation of the great and multiple program outlined by the Second Vatican Council.

The Church, in order that she may carry out her mission with regard to the "world," must strengthen herself deeply in her own mystery, and must construct thoroughly her own community, the community of the People of God, based on the apostolic succession, on the hierarchical ministry, on the vocation to exclusive service of God in the priesthood and in religious life, and on the laity aware of its own apostolic tasks.

The Latin-American world is waiting for the Church to carry out her own mission with regard to it. It is waiting for it even when it shows contestation and indifference with regard to the Church and the Gospel.

All this must not discourage the apostles of Christ and the servants of the Gospel of His love.

My dear brothers in the episcopate of the Latin-American continent are bearing witness that "the love of Christ controls us" (cf. 2 Cor. 5:14), that they are ready to "preach the word, be urgent in season and out of season, convince, rebuke, and exhort, be unfailing in patience and in teaching" (cf. 2 Tm. 4:2)—as St. Paul says—in order that the communities, entrusted to their care as pastors and teachers, will not "turn away from listening to the truth and wander into myths" (cf. 2 Tm. 4:4).

My brothers in the episcopate of the Latin-American continent are ready, together with their priests, religious men and women, and all zealous laity, to read the "signs of the times," to form the whole People of God in justice, truth, and love.

May the Lord bless them in all this work of theirs.

May He allow them to see the fruits of this zeal and this cooperation, the proof of which has been the Third General Conference in Puebla.

May the Church in the Latin-American continent, strong in the tradition of its first evangelization, become strong again with the conscience of the whole People of God; with the strength of its own priestly and religious vocations; with a deep sense of responsibility for the social order, based on justice, peace, respect of human rights, on the adequate distribution of goods, on the progress of public education and culture.

We wish them all of this.

Let all of us gathered here, and the whole Church, continue to pray tirelessly for these aims of Latin America, invoking the intercession of the Mother of God of Guadalupe, at whose feet we began our work.

Amen.

Your Commitment of Prayer and Sacrifice

On Ash Wednesday, 1979, on his way back from the ceremony at Santa Sabina Basilica, the Holy Father made a brief stop at the monastery of enclosed Camaldolese nuns. He addressed them as follows:

I am happy, beloved sisters in Christ, at this meeting which you so greatly desired. Addressing an affectionate greeting to you, I wish to remind you with what great motherly solicitude the Church looks to your commitment of prayer, contemplation, and sacrifice.

To attend to God is considered by the masters of spiritual life to be the most noble and lofty form of activity of the human being, in that the latter concentrates the whole of himself in worshiping and listening to the Infinite Being, who desires the salvation of all mankind. It is understandable, then, how this prayer of praise is accompanied by prayer of propitiation and supplication in order that the divine will may be accomplished.

And the more innocent and pure the soul that presents the prayer, the more acceptable it is to God. Here, then, is the precious form of collaboration that you, enclosed nuns of eminently contemplative life, offer to the Church for the good of souls.

Not only do I ask you to persevere in your generous resolutions, but I exhort you to advance more and more in friendship with God, to stir up continually the flame of love, as it were, volcanoes covered with snow. In the present time with all its difficulties, may your prayer, nourished by sacrifice in solitude and silence, draw God's merciful goodness upon the earth. And with this wish I invoke divine assistance on the whole community and I bless you paternally.

The Vocation to Service and Kingship

The following is an excerpt from the encyclical letter Redemptor hominis *of Pope John Paul II to his venerable brothers in the episcopate, the priests, the religious families, the sons, the daughters of the Church, and to all men and women of good will at the beginning of his papal ministry, issued March 4, 1979.*

In presenting the complete picture of the People of God and recalling the place among that people held not only by priests but also by the laity, not only by the representatives of the hierarchy but also by those of the institutes of consecrated life, the Second Vatican Council did not deduce this picture merely from a sociological premise. The Church as a human society can of course be examined and described according to the categories used by the sciences with regard to any human society. But these categories are not enough. For the whole of the community of the People of God and for each member of it what is in question is not just a specific "social membership"; rather, for each and every one what is essential is a particular "vocation." Indeed, the Church as the People of God is also—according to the teaching of St. Paul mentioned above, of which Pius XII reminded us in wonderful terms—"Christ's Mystical Body." Membership in that body has for its source a particular call, united with the saving action of grace. Therefore, if we wish to keep in mind this community of the People of God, which is so vast and so extremely differentiated, we must see first and foremost Christ saying in a way to each member of the community: "Follow me." It is the community of the disciples, each of whom in a different way—at times very consciously and consistently, at other times not very consciously and very inconsistently—is following Christ. This shows also the deeply "personal" aspect and dimension of this society, which, in spite of all the deficiencies of its community life—in the human meaning of this word—is a community precisely because all its members form it together with Christ Himself, at least because they bear in their souls the indelible mark of a Christian.

The Second Vatican Council devoted very special attention to showing how this "ontological" community of disciples and confessors must increasingly become, even from the "human" point of view, a community aware of its own life and activity. The initiatives taken by the Council in this field have been followed up by the many further initiatives of a synodal, apostolic and organizational kind. We must however always keep in mind the truth that every initiative serves true renewal in the Church and helps to bring the authentic light that is Christ insofar as the initiative is based on adequate awareness of the individual Christian's vocation and of responsibility for this singular, unique and unrepeatable grace by which each Christian in the community of the People of God builds up the Body of Christ. This principle, the key rule for the whole of Christian practice—apostolic and pastoral practice, practice of interior and of social life—must with due proportion be applied to the whole of humanity and to each human being. The Pope too and every bishop must apply this principle to himself. Priests and religious must be faithful to this principle. It is the basis on which their lives must be built by married people, parents, and women and men of different conditions and professions, from those who occupy the highest posts in society to those who perform the simplest tasks. It is precisely the principle of the ''kingly service'' that imposes on each one of us, in imitation of Christ's example, the duty to demand of himself exactly what we have been called to, what we have personally obliged ourselves to by God's grace, in order to respond to our vocation. This fidelity to the vocation received from God through Christ involves the joint responsibility for the Church for which the Second Vatican Council wishes to educate all Christians. Indeed, in the Church as the community of the People of God under the guidance of the Holy Spirit's working, each member has ''his own special gift,'' as St. Paul teaches. Although this ''gift'' is a personal vocation and a form of participation in the Church's saving work, it also serves others and builds the Church and the fraternal communities in the various spheres of human life on earth.

Fidelity to one's vocation, that is to say persevering readiness for ''kingly service,'' has particular significance for these many forms of building, especially with regard to the more exigent tasks, which have more influence on the life of our neighbor and that of the whole of society. Married people must be distinguished for fidelity to their vocation, as is demanded by the indissoluble nature of the sacramental institution of marriage. Priests must be distinguished for a similar fidelity to their vocation, in view of the indelible character that the sacrament of Orders stamps on their souls. In receiving this sacrament, we in the Latin Church knowingly and freely commit ourselves to live in celibacy, and each one of us must therefore do all he can, with God's grace, to be thankful for this gift and faithful to the bond that he has accepted for ever. He must do so as married people must, for they must endeavor with all their strength to persevere in their matrimonial union, building up the family community through this witness of love and educating new generations of men and women, capable in their turn of dedicating the whole of their lives to their vocation, that is to say to the "kingly service" of which Jesus Christ has offered us the example and the most beautiful model. His Church, made up of all of us, is "for men" in the sense that, by basing ourselves on Christ's example and collaborating with the grace that He has gained for us, we are able to attain to "being kings," that is to say, we are able to produce a mature humanity in each one of us. Mature humanity means full use of the gift of freedom received from the Creator when He called to existence the man made "in his image, after his likeness." This gift finds its full realization in the unreserved giving of the whole of one's human person, in a spirit of the love of a spouse, to Christ and, with Christ, to all those to whom He sends men and women totally consecrated to Him in accordance with the evangelical counsels. This is the ideal of the religious life, which has been undertaken by the orders and congregations both ancient and recent, and by the secular institutes.

Nowadays it is sometimes held, though wrongly, that freedom is an end in itself, that each human being is free when he makes use of freedom as he wishes, and that this must be our aim in the lives of individuals and societies. In reality, freedom is a great gift only when we know how to use it consciously for everything that is our true good. Christ teaches us that the best use of freedom is charity, which takes concrete form in self-giving and in service. For this "freedom Christ has set us free" and ever continues to set us free. The Church draws from this source the unceasing inspiration, the call and the drive for her mission and her service among all mankind. The full truth about human freedom is indelibly inscribed on the mystery of the Redemption. The Church truly serves mankind when she guards this truth with untiring attention, fervent love and mature commitment and when in the whole of her own community she transmits it and gives it concrete form in human life through each Christian's fidelity to his vocation. This confirms what we have already referred to, namely that man is and always becomes the "way" for the Church's daily life (no. 21).

Migrations: The Commitment of the Church

On March 14, 1979, Pope John Paul II delivered an address to participants in the World Congress on Problems of the Phenomenon of Migration. The following is an excerpt.

An indefatigable effort must...be made to drive home to Churches of origin and the host Churches the needs of migrants. Do the Churches of origin take enough care to accompany their "diaspora," to prepare "missionaries" for them, and to sustain them? And do the host Churches, sometimes very pressed, pay enough attention to the presence of migrants? Do they take the means that this apostolate requires? Do they see to it, particularly, that priests, religious, and laity dedicate themselves in priority to these environments, which are often relegated to the fringes of society?

Let us make it quite clear: the apostolate of migrants is not just the work of these detached "missionaries": it is the work of the whole local Church, priests, religious and laity; it is the whole local Church which must take migrants into account, and be ready for welcome and for mutual exchanges. In particular, when it is a question of promoting the integration of foreigners, of providing for their human needs and their social advancement, of allowing them to exercise their temporal responsibilities, priests have not to take the place of laity of the host country, nor, on the other hand, these latter the place of the immigrants. But the "missionaries" still play an essential part, precisely to educate both sides to their own role, and they have a special contribution to make for the religious vitality of the communities of migrants. Their task is, moreover, a difficult one and your world congress was right to stress the formation and duties of these "missionaries."

Catholic Education

On the occasion of the annual convention of the National Catholic Educational Association of the United States, which convened in Philadelphia on April 16, 1979, the Holy Father sent the following message to the Association.

Praised be Jesus Christ!

It is a joy for me to address the members of the National Catholic Educational Association of the United States, as you assemble in the great cause of Catholic education. Through you I would hope that my message of encouragement and blessing would also reach the numerous Catholic schools in your country, all the students and teachers of these institutions and all those generously committed to Catholic education. With the apostle Peter I send you my greeting in the faith of our Lord Jesus Christ: "Peace to all of you who are in Christ" (1 Pt. 5:14).

As Catholic educators assembled in the communion of the universal Church and in prayer, you will certainly share with each other insights of value that will assist you in your important work, in your ecclesial mission. The Holy Spirit is with you and the Church is deeply grateful for your dedication. The Pope speaks to you in order to confirm you in your lofty role as Catholic educators, to assist you, to direct you, to support you.

Among the many reflections that could be made at this time there are three points in particular to which I would like to make a brief reference at the beginning of my pontificate. These are: *the value of Catholic schools, the importance of Catholic teachers and educators,* and *the nature of Catholic education itself.* These are themes that have been developed at length by my predecessors. At this time, however, it is important that I add my own testimony to theirs, in the special hope of giving a new impulse to Catholic education throughout the vast area of the United States of America.

With profound conviction I ratify and reaffirm the words that Paul VI spoke originally to the bishops of your country: "Brethren, we know the difficulties involved in preserving Catholic schools, and the uncertainties of the future, and yet we rely on the help of God and on your own zealous collaboration and untiring efforts, so that Catholic schools can continue, despite grave obstacles, to fulfill their providential role at the service of genuine Catholic education, and at the service of your country" (Address of September 15, 1975). Yes, the Catholic school must remain *a privileged means of Catholic education in America.* As an instrument of the apostolate it is worthy of the greatest sacrifices.

But no Catholic school can be effective without dedicated Catholic teachers, convinced of the great ideal of Catholic education. The Church needs men and women who are intent on teaching by word and example—intent on helping to permeate the whole educational milieu with the spirit of Christ. This is a great vocation, and the Lord Himself will reward all who serve in it as educators in the cause of the Word of God.

In order that the Catholic school and Catholic teachers may truly make their irreplaceable contribution to the Church and to the world, the goal of Catholic education itself must be crystal clear. Beloved sons and daughters of the Catholic Church, brothers and sisters in the faith: Catholic education is above all a question of communicating Christ, of helping to form Christ in the lives of others. In the expression of the Second Vatican Council, those who have been baptized must be made ever more aware of the gift of faith that they have received, they must learn to adore the Father in spirit and in truth, and they must be trained to live the newness of Christian life in justice and in the holiness of truth (cf. *Gravissimum educationis*, no. 2).

These are indeed essential aims of Catholic education. To foster and promote them gives meaning to the Catholic school; it spells out the dignity of the vocation of Catholic educators.

Yes, it is above all a question of communicating Christ, and helping His uplifting Gospel to take root in the hearts of the faithful. Be strong, therefore, in pursuing these goals. The cause of Catholic education is the cause of Jesus Christ and of His Gospel at the service of man.

And be assured of the solidarity of the entire Church, and of the sustaining grace of our Lord Jesus Christ. In His name, I send you all my apostolic blessing: in the name of the Father, and of the Son, and of the Holy Spirit. Amen.

Formation of Catechists

*During the general audience on April 25, 1979, the
Holy Father gave the following brief address to those
who had been taking part in the International Council for Catechesis.*

I now wish to address a special greeting to
members of the International Council for Catechesis, composed of bishops, priests, sisters and
lay experts, who have met here in Rome in these
days to examine the important subject of the
"Formation of Catechists," and who, together
with the superiors and some officials of the
Sacred Congregation for the Clergy, which
organized the meeting, have come here to express to the Pope their ecclesial communion.

I thank you, dear brothers, for this significant presence of yours and, even more, for your
active commitment in updating the delicate and
important sector of catechesis, which is certainly
the *opus princeps* of the Church's mission.
The theme you have chosen is too vast and important for me to be able to refer to it here: I will
limit myself, therefore, to a short and simple exhortation. I am of the opinion that in the catechist's formation, over and above all problems
regarding the content and the method of teaching, uprightness of life and sincerity of Christian
faith are necessary. Neither cultural preparation
nor pedagogical skill are sufficient to make the
revealed truths accessible to the mentality of
modern man. These are necessary things, but
they are not enough: the catechist must have a

soul which lives and brings life to everything he professes. In this connection I am glad to leave you, as an inspiring motive, some expressions of St. Bonaventure of Bagnoregio, who, in his *Itinerarium mentis in Deum* admonished the teachers of his time, with sculptural clarity, as follows: *Nemo credat quod sibi sufficiat lectio sine unctione, speculatio sine devotione, investigatio sine admiratione, circumspectio sine exultatione, industria sine pietate, scientia sine caritate, intelligentia sine humilitate, studium- absque divina gratia, speculum absque sapientia divinitus inspirata* (Introduction, no. 4).*

All that demands of the catechist, of course, great love for Jesus Christ, our Master. It demands readiness to listen to His voice and follow Him daily in order to be able to learn how He spoke, in His continual catechesis, to children, to the young, to the learned and to the ignorant.

This is, dear brothers, the brief thought I wished to express to you. May the Holy Spirit sustain you in your work, and the Blessed Virgin, *Sedis Sapientiae*, encourage you in difficulties. To all of you my fatherly blessing, which I willingly bestow also on all those who are engaged in various capacities in the delicate field of catechesis.

---

*Let no one believe that it is enough to give a lecture without affecting the students, to speculate without devotion, to investigate without admiration, to be prudent without a pleasant disposition, to be zealous without piety, to have knowledge without charity, intelligence without humility, diligence without divine grace; to be a mirror without divinely inspired wisdom.

Service and the Eucharist

The Holy Father received on April 26, 1979, a group of thirteen bishops of India on their ad limina Apostolorum visit. The bishops, coming from Bengal and the northeast section of the country were led by His Eminence Cardinal Trevor Lawrence Picachy, Archbishop of Calcutta. Pope John Paul delivered a discourse to the group. The following is an excerpt.

The effectiveness of the laity, and in particular of Christian families, to give to the world the witness of faith and love is conditioned by their spiritual dynamism, which is nowhere more available than in the Eucharist. The youth of your local Churches can only come to full maturity in Christ through the power of the Eucharist. God's gift of priestly and religious vocations is mysteriously related to the reverent participation of God's people in the Eucharist....

Our ministry is indeed a ministry of faith, and the supernatural means to effect our goal are commensurate with the wisdom and power of God. *The Eucharist and Penance are great treasures of Christ's Church.*

In all the challenges and joys of our ministry, in all our hopes and disappointments, in all the difficulties inherent in proclaiming Christ and His uplifting message for the cause of man and human dignity, let us reflect, in faith, that *Christ's power, and not our own, guides our steps and supports our efforts.* Today, in the fraternity of collegiality that is ours we can hear

Christ speaking to us: *Ecce ego vobiscum sum.*
And when you return to your people, endeavor to
communicate the same message of faith, confidence and strength to the whole community—to
the priests, religious and laity who make up with
you the People of God: *Ecce ego vobiscum sum.*
Particularly in the Eucharist.

To Win Over the Minds and Hearts of the Young

On April 29, 1979, the Holy Father preached the following homily during the beatification ceremony of Father Jacques Laval, C.S.Sp., and Father Francis Coll, O.P.

Dear brothers and sisters,

1. Alleluia! Alleluia! On this third Sunday of Easter, our paschal joy is expressed as an echo of the overflowing joy of the Apostles who, from the first day, recognized the risen Christ. On Easter evening, "Jesus himself stood among them." "See my hands and my feet." He invited them to touch Him with their hands. And He ate before their eyes (cf. Lk. 24:36, 39, 40). Amazed and slow to believe, the Apostles recognized Him at last: "The disciples were glad when they saw the Lord" (Jn. 20:20; Lk. 24:41); and now no one could take their joy from them (cf. Jn. 16:22), or silence their testimony (cf. Acts 4:20). A few moments earlier, the hearts of the disciples of Emmaus were also burning within them while Jesus spoke to them on the way and explained the Scriptures to them; and they too had recognized Him at the breaking of bread (cf. Lk. 24:32, 35).

The joy of these witnesses is ours, dear brothers and sisters, we who share their faith in the risen Christ. Glorified at the Father's side, He never stops drawing men to Him, communicating to them His life, the Spirit of holiness, while preparing a place for them in the Father's house. Today, as it happens, this joy finds a striking confirmation, since we are honoring two admirable Servants of God who, last century, shone forth on our earth with Christ's holiness and whom the Church is now able to declare Blessed, to propose them to the special veneration and imitation of the faithful: Father Laval·and Father Coll, whom we must now contemplate.

EVANGELIZATION OF THE POOR

2. It is plainly impossible to point out here all the outstanding events in the life of Father Jacques-Désiré Laval, or all the Christian virtues that he practiced to a heroic degree. Let us remember at least what characterizes this missionary, with regard to the mission of the Church today.

It is in the first place his concern to evangelize the poor, the poorest, and, in this case, his "dear Blacks" of the island of Mauritius, as he used to call them. A Frenchman, he had begun by practicing medicine in a little town in his native diocese, Evreux, but gradually the call to an undivided love of the Lord, which he had repressed for a certain time, made him abandon his profession and worldly life. "Once I am a priest, I will be able to do more good," he explained to his brother (cf. biography).

A late vocation at St. Sulpice Seminary in Paris, he was at once put in charge of service of the poor; then, as parish priest of the little Norman parish of Pinterville, he shared all he had with those in want. But on learning of the misery of the Blacks of Africa and the urgency of bringing them to Christ, he obtained permission to leave for the island of Mauritius, with the Vicar Apostolic, Bishop Collier. For twenty-three years, until his death, he dedicated all his time, used all his strength, and gave his whole heart to the evangelization of the inhabitants: indefatigably, he listened to them, catechized them, and made them discover their Christian vocation. He often intervened also to improve their medical and social condition.

His tenaciousness is an unending source of astonishment for us, especially in the discouraging conditions of his mission. But, in his apostolate, he always went to what was essential.

The fact is that our missionary left behind him innumerable converts, with a firm faith and piety. He was not given to sensational ceremonies, fascinating for these simple souls but with no lasting effect, or to flights of oratory. His educational concern was closely integrated in life. He was not afraid to return continually to the essential points of Christian doctrine and practice, and he admitted to Baptism or to First Communion only people prepared in little groups and tested. He took great care to put at the disposal of the faithful little chapels scattered over the island. Another remarkable initiative which links up with the concern of many pastors today: he had recourse to collaborators, men and women, as leaders of prayer, catechists, people who visited and advised the sick, others in charge of little Christian communities, in other words, poor people, evangelizers of the poor.

What is, then, the secret of his missionary zeal? We find it in his holiness: in the gift of his whole person to Jesus Christ, inseparable from his tender love of men, especially the most humble among them, to whom he wished to give access to the salvation of Christ. Whatever time was not dedicated to the direct apostolate, he spent in prayer, especially before the Blessed Sacrament, and he continually combined with prayer mortifications and acts of penance which deeply impressed his confreres, in spite of his discretion and his humility.

He himself often expressed regret for his spiritual lukewarmness—let us say rather the feeling of his aridity: is it not precisely that he set the greatest store by fervent love of God and Mary, to which he wished to initiate his faithful? That is also the secret of his apostolic patience: "It is on God alone and on the protection of the Blessed Virgin that we depend" (Letter of July 6, 1833, cf. biography). What a magnificent confession! His missionary spirituality had been, from the beginning, in keeping with the general pattern of a young religious and Marian institute, and he was always anxious to follow its spiritual requirements, in spite of his solitude and geographical distance: the Society of the Sacred Heart of Mary, of which he was one of the first members alongside the famous Father Libermann, and which was soon to merge with the Congregation of the Holy Spirit. The apostle, now as in the past, must in the first place maintain spiritual vigor within himself: he bears witness that he is continually drawing from the Source.

That is a model for evangelizers today. May he inspire missionaries and, I venture to say, all priests, who have in the first place the sublime mission of proclaiming Jesus Christ and training the Christian life!

May he be, in a special way, the joy and stimulus of all religious of the Holy Spirit, who have never stopped implanting the Church, particularly in the land of Africa, and are at work there so generously!

May the example of Father Laval encourage all of those who, on the African continent and elsewhere, are endeavoring to build a brotherly world, free of racial prejudices! May Blessed Laval be also the pride, the ideal and the protector of the Christian community of the island of Mauritius, so dynamic today, and of all Mauritians!

To these wishes, I am happy to add a very cordial greeting to the delegation of the government of Mauritius, as well as to that of the French government, which have come to take part in this ceremony.

FATHER FRANCIS COLL

3. A second reason for ecclesial joy is the beatification of another figure that the Church wishes to exalt today and propose to the imitation of the People of God: Father Francis Coll. A new glory of the great Dominican family and equally so, of the diocesan family of Vich. A religious and at the same time a model apostle—for a large part of his life—in the ranks of the clergy of Vich.

He is one of those ecclesial personalities who, in the second half of the nineteenth century, enriched the Church with new religious foundations; a son of Spain, of Catalonia, which has produced so many generous souls that have bequeathed a fruitful heritage to the Church.

In our case, this heritage takes on concrete form in a magnificent and tireless work of evangelical preaching, which culminates in the foundation of the institute known today as that of the Dominican Sisters of "La Anunciata," present here in large numbers to celebrate their Father Founder, together with so many members of the various organizations which the congregation has created.

We cannot now present a complete portrait of the new Blessed, an admirable mirror—as you have been able to observe from a reading of his biography—of heroic human, Christian and religious virtues, which make him worthy of praise and of imitation in our earthly pilgrimage. Let us merely speak briefly about one of the most striking aspects of this ecclesial figure.

What impresses us most on approaching the life of the new Blessed is his evangelizing zeal. At a very difficult moment of history, in which social upheavals and laws persecuting the Church made him leave his convent and live permanently outside it, Father Coll, abstracting from human, sociological or political considerations, dedicated himself completely to an astonishing task of preaching. Both during his parish ministry, especially in Artés y Moya, and in his later phase as an apostolic missionary,

Father Coll showed himself to be a true catechist, an evangelizer, in the best line of the Order of Preachers.

In his innumerable apostolic journeys over the whole of Catalonia, through memorable popular missions and other forms of preaching, Father Coll—Mosén Coll, for many—was a transmitter of faith, a sower of hope, a preacher of love, peace and reconciliation among those whom passions, war and hatred kept divided. A real man of God, he lived fully his priestly and religious identity, made a source of inspiration in the whole of his task. To those who did not always understand the reasons for certain attitudes of his, he answered with a convinced "because I am a religious." This deep consciousness of himself was what directed his incessant labor.

An absorbing task, but which did not lack a solid foundation: frequent prayer, which was the driving power of his apostolic activity. On this point, the new Blessed speaks very eloquently. He himself is a man of prayer; he wishes to introduce the faithful along this way (it is enough to see what he says in two publications of his *La hermosa rosa* and *La escala del cielo*). It is the path he points out in the Rule to his daughters, with stirring words, which because of their relevance today I also make my own: "The life of sisters must be a life of prayer.... For this reason I urge you over and over again, beloved sisters: do not abandon prayer."

The new Blessed recommends various forms of prayer to sustain apostolic activity. But there is one that he prefers and which I have particular pleasure in mentioning and emphasizing: prayer while contemplating the mysteries of the rosary; that "ladder to go up to heaven," composed of mental and vocal prayer which "are the two wings that Mary's rosary offers Christian souls." A form of prayer which the Pope too practices assiduously and in which he calls upon all of you to join, particularly in the coming month of May, dedicated to the Virgin.

I conclude these reflections in Spanish with a greeting to the authorities who have come for these celebrations in honor of Father Coll. I invite everyone to imitate his example of life, but especially the sons of St. Dominic, the clergy and particularly you, Dominican Sisters of the "Anunciata," who have come from Spain, Europe, America and Africa, where your religious activity is carried on generously.

DEFINITE PRIORITY OF CATECHESIS

4. The hope that I express this morning, in conclusion, is that today's double Beatification will serve to strengthen and promote commitment in the catechetical action of the whole Church. It is well known that the subject of the Fourth General Assembly of the Synod of Bishops, held here in Rome in the autumn of 1977, was precisely that of catechesis. The Synod Fathers—of whom I too was one—tackled and studied this theme of prime importance for the life and action of the Church at all times. They stressed the urgency of giving catechesis definite priority over other initiatives, less essential even if, perhaps, more spectacular, because the ab-

solutely original aspect of the Church's mission is carried out by means of it. A mission—they confirmed—which involves all members of the People of God, though in their different functions, and commits them to a continual search for adequate methods and means for a more and more effective transmission of the message.

The thought of the Synod Fathers was addressed particularly to the young, of whose growing importance in the world of today they were well aware: for amid uncertainties and disorders, excesses and frustrations, the young represent the great force on which the fate of future humanity depends. The question that troubled the Synod Fathers is precisely this one: how to get this multitude of young people to have a living experience of Jesus Christ, and that not just in the dazzling encounter of a fleeting moment, but by means of a knowledge of His Person and His message that becomes more complete and luminous every day? How to kindle in them the passion for the kingdom, which He came to inaugurate, and in which alone the human being can find full and satisfying self-fulfillment?

To answer this question is the most urgent task of the Church today. It will depend on the generous commitment of all, if a testimony of the "message of this salvation" (Acts 13:26) can be offered to the new generations, a testimony capable of winning over the minds and hearts of the young, and of involving their will in those concrete choices, often costly ones, which the logic of the love of God and of one's neighbor demands. I will depend above all on the sincerity and the intensity with which families and communities are able to live their adherence to Christ, if the young are effectively reached by the teachings imparted to them at home, in school, in church.

Let us pray, therefore, the new Blesseds to be close to us with their intercession and to guide us to personal and deep experience of the risen Christ, who will make our hearts also "burn within us," as the hearts of the two disciples burned on the way to Emmaus, while Jesus "talked to them on the road and opened to them the Scriptures" (cf. Lk. 24:32). In fact, only he who can say: "I know him"—and St. John has warned us that anyone who does not live according to Christ's commandments cannot say this (cf. Second Reading)—only he who has reached an "existential" knowledge of Him and of His Gospel, can offer others a credible, incisive and enthralling catechesis.

The lives of the two new Blesseds are an eloquent confirmation of this. May their example not be proposed to us in vain!

An Example to All

On April 30, 1979, the Holy Father presided over a solemn Eucharistic concelebration for the Croat National Pilgrimage, which brought to Rome over eight thousand faithful from Croatia and the major countries of Croat emigration.

Cardinals Seper and Bertoli, and the thirteen Croat bishops who led the pilgrimage, celebrated with the Pope. John Paul II delivered the homily in Croat. The following is an excerpt.

While I raise my hands today to bless you who are present, the whole of your people and the whole of your land, I beg the Lord to preserve your faith and I implore the Mother of God to be always and everywhere "your powerful advocate." I extend my blessing to your bishops, priests, men and women religious, in order that, faithful to their own vocation, they may be an example to all, and not go astray (Letter from Pope John VIII to the Bishop of Nin, Theodosius, *Mansi,* l.c. XVII, 124), but may announce the Gospel of Christ as a joyful message of salvation, truth, love and concord. I bless all of you present, your families, young and old, workers and intellectuals, and I beg you: remain faithful to God and to Peter, foster a good family spirit, respect life, bring up a more and more numerous youth and keep the noble tradition of family prayer. I address, above all, you, young faithful: know and love Jesus Christ, man's only Redeemer, and be proud of your Christian name.

The World Needs Consecrated Souls

On the afternoon of May 1, 1979, the Holy Father visited the Sanctuary of Divine Love on the outskirts of Rome. Before beginning Mass, John Paul II addressed the congregation. An excerpt follows.

In this spiritual atmosphere of Marian piety, on next Sunday is celebrated the day of prayer for ecclesiastical vocations, whether priestly or simply religious. The Church gives great importance to this day, at a moment when the problem of vocations is at the center of the deepest concerns and cares of the ecclesial apostolate. Kindly put this intention in your prayers during the whole month of May. Today, more than ever, the world needs priests and religious, sisters, consecrated souls to meet the immense needs of men. There are children and young people who are waiting for someone to teach them the way to salvation; there are men and women whose heavy daily work makes them feel more acutely the need of God; there are old, sick and suffering people, who are waiting for someone to bend over their tribulations and open up to them the hope of heaven. It is a duty of the Christian people to ask God, through the intercession of our Lady, to send workers to His harvest (cf. Mt. 9:38), by making very many young people listen to His voice stimulating their consciences to supernatural values and making them understand and evaluate, in all its beauty, the gift of this call.

Mary Is with Us as a Mother

On May 2, 1979, at the general audience in St. Peter's Square, Pope John Paul II addressed the faithful. An excerpt follows.

I wish in particular to bring the youth of the whole world and of the whole Church closer to her, to Mary who is the Mother of fair love. She bears within her an indestructible sign of youth and beauty which never pass. I wish and pray that the young will approach her, have confidence in her, and entrust to her the life that is before them; that they will love her with a simple and warm love of the heart. She alone is capable of responding to this love in the best way:

Ipsam sequens non devias,
ipsam rogans non desperas,
ipsam cogitans non erras...
ipsam propitia—pervenis...

(St. Bernard, *Homilia II super Missus est,* XVII: *PL* 183, 71).

To Mary who is the Mother of divine grace I entrust priestly and religious vocations. May the new spring of vocations, their new increase throughout the Church, become a particular proof of her motherly presence in the mystery of Christ, in our times, and in the mystery of His Church all over the earth. Mary alone is a living incarnation of that total and complete dedication to God, to Christ, to His salvific action, which must find its adequate expression in every priestly and religious vocation. Mary is the fullest expression of perfect faithfulness to the Holy Spirit and to His action in the soul; she is the expression of the faithfulness which means persevering cooperation in the grace of vocation.

Next Sunday is appointed in the whole Church to prayer for vocations to the priesthood and for vocations of men and women to the religious life. It is Vocation Sunday. Through the intercession of the Mother of divine grace, may it bring an abundant harvest.

Three Passwords: Pray, Call, Respond

The following is the message of Pope John Paul II for the Sixteenth World Day of Prayer for Vocations, on May 6, 1979.

Dear brothers in the episcopate,
Dear sons and daughters throughout the world,

This is the first time that the new Pope is speaking to you on the occasion of the World Day of Prayer for Vocations.

In the first place, let my and your affectionate and grateful remembrance go to the late Pope Paul VI. We are grateful, because during the Council he established this day of prayer for all vocations to special consecration to God and the Church. We are grateful, because every year, for fifteen years, he highlighted this day with his words as a teacher, and encouraged us with his pastor's heart.

Following his example, I now turn to you on this Sixteenth World Day, to confide to you a number of things that I have very much at heart, almost like three passwords: pray, call, respond.

PRAY FOR LABORERS

1. First of all, *pray.* The reason why we must pray is certainly a big one, if Christ Himself commanded us to do it: "Pray therefore the Lord of the harvest to send out laborers into his harvest" (Mt. 9:38). Let this day be a public witness of

faith and obedience to the Lord's command. So celebrate it in your Cathedrals: the bishops together with the clergy, the men and women religious, the missionaries, those aspiring to the priesthood and the consecrated life, the people, the young people, many young people. Celebrate it in the parishes, communities, shrines, colleges and the places where there are people who are suffering. From every part of the world let this insistent prayer rise to heaven, to ask the Father what Christ wanted us to ask.

A DAY FULL OF HOPE

Let it be a day full of hope. May it find us gathered together, as though in a worldwide Upper Room, "in continuous prayer, together with...Mary the Mother of Jesus" (Acts 1:14), confidently awaiting the gifts of the Holy Spirit. In fact, on the altar of the Eucharistic Sacrifice, round which we gather in prayer, it is the same Christ who prays with us and for us, and assures us that we shall obtain what we ask for: "If two of you agree on earth about anything you ask, it will be done for you by my Father in heaven. For where two or three are gathered in my name, there am I in the midst of them" (Mt. 18:19f.). There are many of us gathered in His name, and we ask only for what He wants. In view of His solemn promise, how can we fail to pray with minds full of hope?

Let this day be a center of spiritual radiation. Let our prayer spread out and continue in the churches, communities, families, the hearts of the faithful, as though in an invisible monastery from which an unbroken invocation rises to the Lord.

"COME, FOLLOW ME!"

2. *Call.* I would now like to speak to you, brothers in the episcopate, and to your collaborators in the priesthood, in order to strengthen and encourage you in the ministry which you are already laudably exercising. Let us be faithful to the Council, which exhorted bishops to "foster priestly and religious vocations as much as possible, and take a special interest in missionary vocations" (*Christus Dominus,* no. 15).

Christ, who commanded prayer for the laborers in the harvest, has also personally called those laborers. The words of His call are preserved in the treasure of the Gospel: "Follow me, and I will make you fishers of men" (Mt. 4:19). "Come, follow me" (Mt. 19:21). "If anyone serves me, he must follow me" (Jn. 12:26). The words of His call are entrusted to our apostolic ministry and we must make them heard, like the other words of the Gospel, "to the end of the earth" (Acts 1:8). It is Christ's will that we should make them heard. The People of God have a right to hear them from us.

The admirable pastoral programs of the individual Churches, the organizations for vocations that, in accordance with the Council, have the task of promoting all pastoral activity for vocations (cf. Decree *Optatam totius,* no. 2), open the way and prepare the good ground for the Lord's grace. God is always free to call whom

He wishes and when He wishes, in accordance with "the immeasurable riches of his grace in kindness towards us in Christ Jesus" (Eph. 2:7). But usually He calls by means of us and our words. So, do not be afraid to call. Go among your young people. Go and meet them personally and call them. The hearts of many young people, and not-so-young people, are ready to listen to you. Many of them are looking for something to live for; they are waiting to discover a worthwhile mission, to devote their lives to it. Christ has attuned them to His call and yours. We must call. The Lord will do the rest, He who offers each individual his or her special gift, according to the grace that has been given to that person (cf. 1 Cor. 7:7; Rom. 12:6).

Let us carry out this ministry wholeheartedly. Let us open our minds, as the Council wishes, "to transcend the boundaries of each diocese, nation, religious community, and rite. Responding to the needs of the whole Church, special help should be given to those places where workers for the Lord's vineyard are more urgently called for" (Decree *Optatam totius,* no. 2). What I have said to the bishops and their cooperators in the priestly order I would also like to say to religious superiors, to the heads of secular institutes, and to the leaders of missionary life, so that each one can play his or her part, according to individual responsibilities, with a view to the general good of the Church.

3. *Respond.* I am speaking in a special way to you, the young people. In fact I would like to talk with you, with each one of you. You are very dear

to me and I have great confidence in you. I have called you the hope of the Church and my hope.

Let us remind ourselves of a few things together. In the treasure of the Gospel there are preserved the beautiful responses given to the Lord when He called. The response of Peter and Andrew his brother: "Immediately they left their nets and followed him" (Mt. 4:20). The response of Levi the publican: "And he left everything, and rose and followed him" (Lk. 5:28). The response of the Apostles: "Lord, to whom shall we go? You have the words of eternal life" (Jn. 6:68). The response of Saul: "What shall I do, Lord?" (Acts 22:10) From the time when the Gospel was first proclaimed right up to our time, a very large number of men and women have given their personal response, their free and deliberate response, to the call of Christ. They have chosen the priesthood, the religious life, life in the missions, as the reason for and the ideal of existence. They have served the People of God and humanity, with faith, intelligence, courage and love. Now it is time for you. It is up to you to respond. Are you afraid, perhaps?

OUR LIFE A GIFT

Then let us reflect together, in the light of faith. Our life is a gift from God. We must do something good with it. There are many ways of living life well, using it for serving human and Christian ideals. My reason for speaking to you today about total dedication to God in the priesthood, in the religious life, in life as a missionary, is that Christ calls many from among you to this extraordinary adventure. He needs, and He wants to need, your persons, your intelligence, your energy, your faith, your love, your holiness. If it is to the priesthood that Christ is calling you, it is because He wishes to exercise His priesthood through your dedication and priestly mission. He wants to speak to the people of today through your voice. He wants to consecrate the Eucharist and forgive sins through you. He wants to love with your heart. He wants to help with your hands. He wants to save through your efforts. Think about it carefully. The response that many of you can give is given personally to Christ, who is calling you to these great things.

THE WORK OF LOVE

You will meet difficulties. Do you think perhaps that I do not know about them? I am telling you that love overcomes all difficulties. The true response to every vocation is the work of love. The response to the priestly, religious and missionary vocation can only spring from a deep love of Christ. He Himself offers you this power of love, as a gift that is added to the gift of His call and makes your response possible. Trust in "him who by the power at work within us is able to do far more abundantly than all that we wish or think" (Eph. 3:20). And, if you can, give your life, with joy and without fear, to Him who first gave His for you.

For this reason I ask you to pray like this:

"Lord Jesus, who called the ones You wanted to call, call many of us to work for You, to work with You.

"You who enlightened with Your words those whom You called, enlighten us with faith in You.

"You who supported them in their difficulties, help us to conquer the difficulties we have as young people today.

"And if You call one of us to be consecrated completely to You, may Your love give warmth to this vocation from its very beginning and make it grow and persevere to the end. Amen."

I entrust these wishes and this prayer to the powerful intercession of Mary, Queen of Apostles, in the hope that those who are called will be able to discern and follow generously the voice of the Divine Master, and I invoke upon you, dear brothers in the episcopate, and upon you, dear sons and daughters of the whole Church, the gifts of the Redeemer's peace and serenity. And with all my heart I impart to you the apostolic blessing....

Following the Example of Jesus, Let Everyone Be a "Good Shepherd"

On May 6, 1979, on the occasion of the World Day of Prayer for Vocations, the Holy Father visited the parish of St. Anthony of Padua at Via Tuscolana, Rome, where he celebrated Mass. John Paul II delivered the following homily.

Beloved brothers and sisters!

Today, in the whole of the Catholic Church, the day for priestly and religious vocations is being observed. I am happy to keep it with you, here in Rome, in the center of Christianity, and in your parish entrusted to the priests of the Congregation of "Rogationists," whom I greet cordially.

This Sunday has been dedicated to this supreme and essential need precisely because the liturgy presents to us the figure of Jesus, the "Good Shepherd."

The Old Testament already usually speaks of God as the Shepherd of Israel, the people of the covenant, chosen by Him to carry out the plan of salvation. Psalm 22 is a marvelous hymn to the Lord, the Shepherd of our soul:

"The Lord is my shepherd, I shall not want;
    he makes me lie down in green pastures,
he leads me beside still waters,
    he restores my soul.
He leads me in paths of righteousness...."

Even though I walk through the valley of the
    shadow of death,
I fear no evil; for you are with me..."
(Ps. 23:1-4).

The prophets Isaiah, Jeremiah, and Ezekiel
often return to the subject of the people as "the
Lord's flock": "Behold your God!... He will feed
his flock like a shepherd, he will gather the lambs
in his arms..." (Is. 40:11). Above all, they announce the Messiah as a Shepherd who will
really feed His sheep and not let them go astray
any more: "I will set up over them one shepherd,
my servant David, and he shall feed them: he
shall feed them and be their shepherd..." (Ez.
34:23).

This sweet and moving figure of the shepherd is a familiar one in the Gospel. Even if times
have changed owing to industrialization and ur-
banism, it always keeps its fascination and effectiveness; and we all remember the touching and
poetic parable of the Good Shepherd who goes in
search of the lost sheep (Lk. 15:3-7).

In the early times of the Church, Christian
iconography used a great deal and developed this
subject of the Good Shepherd, whose image often
appears, painted or sculpted, in the catacombs,
sarcophagi and baptismal fonts. This iconography, so interesting and reverent, testifies to
us that, right from the early times of the Church,
Jesus "the Good Shepherd" struck and moved
the hearts of believers and non-believers, and
was a cause of conversion, spiritual commitment
and comfort. Well, Jesus "the Good Shepherd" is
still alive and true today in our midst, in the

midst of the whole of mankind, and He wants to let each of us hear His voice and feel His love.

1) *What does it mean to be the Good Shepherd?*

Jesus explains it to us with convincing clearness.

—The shepherd knows his sheep and the sheep know him. How wonderful and consoling it is to know that Jesus knows us one by one; that for Him we are not anonymous persons; that our name—that name which is agreed upon by loving parents and friends—is known to Him! For Jesus we are not a "mass," a "multitude"! We are individual "persons" with an eternal value, both as creatures and as redeemed persons! He knows us! He knows me, and loves me and gave Himself for me! (Gal. 2:20).

—The shepherd feeds his sheep and leads them to fresh and abundant pastures. Jesus came to bring life to souls, and to give it in superabundance. And the life of souls consists essentially in three supreme realities: truth, grace, glory. Jesus is the truth, because He is the Word Incarnate. He is the "head of the corner," as St. Peter said to the rulers of the people and elders, the stone on which alone it is possible to construct the family, social, and political edifice: "There is salvation in no one else, for there is no other name under heaven given among men by which we must be saved" (Acts 4:11-12).

Jesus gives us "grace," that is, divine life, by means of Baptism and the other sacraments. Through "grace," we become participants in the very trinitarian nature of God! An immense mystery, but of inexpressible joy and consolation!

Jesus, finally, will give us the glory of paradise, complete and eternal glory, where we will be loved and will love, participants in God's own happiness which is infinite even in joy! "It does not yet appear what we shall be," St. John comments, "but we know that when he appears we shall be like him, for we shall see him as he is" (1 Jn. 3:3).

—The shepherd defends his sheep; he is not like the mercenary who flees when the wolf arrives, because he does not care about the sheep at all. Unfortunately we know very well that there are still mercenaries in the world who sow hatred, malice, doubt, confusion of ideas and of the senses. Jesus, on the contrary, with the light of His divine word and with the strength of His sacramental and ecclesial presence, forms our mind, strengthens the will, purifies sentiments, and thus defends and saves us from so many painful and dramatic experiences.

—Finally, the shepherd feels the desire to increase his flock. Jesus clearly affirms His universal concern: "And I have other sheep, that are not of this fold; I must bring them also, and they will heed my voice. So there shall be one flock, one shepherd" (Jn. 10:16). Jesus wants all men to know Him, love Him and follow Him.

2) *Jesus wanted the priest in the Church as the "Good Shepherd."*

The parish is the Christian community, enlightened by the example of the Good Shepherd, around its own parish priest and priest collaborators.

In the parish the priest continues the mission and the task of Jesus; therefore he must "feed the flock," he must teach, instruct, give grace, defend souls from error and evil, console, help, convert and, above all, love.

Therefore, with all the anxiety of my heart as Pastor of the universal Church I say to you: love your priests! Esteem them, listen to them, follow them! Pray for them every day. Do not leave them alone either at the altar or in daily life!

And never stop praying for priestly vocations and for perseverance in the commitment of consecration to the Lord and to souls. But, above all, create in your families an atmosphere suitable for the flourishing of vocations. And, you parents, be generous in responding to God's plans for your children.

3) *Finally, Jesus wants everyone to be a "good shepherd."*

Every Christian, by virtue of Baptism, is called to be himself a "good shepherd" in the environment in which he lives. You parents must exercise the functions of the Good Shepherd with regard to your children; and you, too, children, must be edifying with your love, your obedience and above all with your courageous and consistent faith. Also the mutual relations between husband and wife must be marked by the example of the Good Shepherd, in order that family life may always have that nobility of sentiments and ideals willed by the Creator, because of which the family has been defined as the "domestic Church." So also at school, at work, in playgrounds and places of leisure, in hospitals and where people are suffering, let everyone always try to be a "good shepherd" like Jesus. But above all let persons consecrated to God, religious, sisters, those who belong to secular institutes, be "good shepherds" in society. Today and always we must pray for all religious vocations, male and female, in order that this testimony of religious life in the Church may be more and more numerous, alive, intense, and always efficacious. Today more than ever the world needs convinced witnesses who are completely consecrated!

Beloved faithful, I conclude by recalling the heartfelt invocation of Jesus the Good Shepherd: "The harvest is plentiful, but the laborers are few; pray therefore the Lord of the harvest to send out laborers into his harvest" (Mt. 9:37; Lk. 10:2).

If only my pastoral visit would bring forth in your parish some priestly vocations among you, young men and boys, innocent and devoted; some religious and missionary vocations among you, young women and girls, blossoming to life, full of enthusiasm!

Let us commend the desire to the Blessed Virgin, the Mother of Jesus the Good Shepherd, our Mother and the inspirer of every sacred vocation!

Let us also invoke the intercession of the Servant of God, Canon Annibale of France, founder of the Congregation of "Rogationists" which, with its vocational center, "Rogate," dedicates its activity mainly to the promotion of priestly and religious vocations.

Love of Those Called
Is the Hope of the Church

On May 6, 1979, the Holy Father addressed the faithful gathered in St. Peter's Square to recite the Marian prayer. The following is an excerpt.

...In this wonderful work [of shepherding souls] Christ does not want to be and to act alone, but He intends to associate with Himself collaborators—men chosen among men in favor of other men (cf. Heb. 5:1). These He calls with a special "vocation" of love, invests with His sacred powers and sends as apostles into the world, so that they may continue His salvific mission, always and everywhere, until the end of time. Christ, therefore, needs, wills to need, the response, the zeal, the love of those who are "called," so that He may still know, guide, defend and love so many other sheep, sacrificing also life for them, if necessary!

And so the Fourth Sunday of Easter recalls, together with the image of the Good Shepherd, also those who are chosen and sent to prolong His mission in time and space (bishops and priests), and it also reminds us of the problem of ecclesiastical vocations, a cause of so much hope and anxiety for the Church. Keeping in mind the fact that—as the Council states—"the task of fostering vocations devolves on the whole Christian community" (Decree *Optatam totius*, no. 2), and considering the urgency and seriousness of this problem, the idea arises spontaneously of connecting Good Shepherd Sunday with the need of having recourse to fervent and confident prayer to the Lord. Prayer, in fact, makes it possible continually to rediscover the dimensions of that kingdom, for the coming of which we pray every day, repeating the words that Christ taught us. Then we realize what our place is in the fulfillment of this supplication: "Thy kingdom come...." When we pray, we shall discover more easily those "fields already white for harvest" (Jn. 4:35) and we will understand the meaning of the words that Christ uttered on seeing them: "Pray therefore the Lord of the harvest to send out laborers into his harvest" (Mt. 9:38).

For the effective and consoling solution to the problem of vocations, the Christian community must, therefore, feel committed in the first place to pray, to pray a great deal, with confidence and perseverance; not neglecting, furthermore, to promote opportune pastoral initiatives and to offer, particularly by means of "consecrated" souls, a luminous testimony of life lived in faithfulness to the divine vocation. We must exert a gentle pressure on the heart of the Lord, who does us the honor of calling us to collaborate with Him for the victory and expansion of His kingdom on earth, in order that "the love of Christ" (2 Cor. 5:14) may awaken the divine call in the hearts of very many young people and in other noble and generous souls, induce the hesitant to make a decision, and sustain in perseverance those who have made their choice in the service of God and of the brethren. May God let everyone fully understand that the presence, the quality, the number and the faithfulness of vocations are a sign of the living and active presence of the Church in the world, and a cause of hope for her future.

I address, finally, a special and cordial appeal to the young. Beloved, look at the ideal represented by the figure of the Good Shepherd—an ideal of light, life and love—and, at the same time, consider that our time needs to refer to such ideals. If Christ's eye dwells on you with predilection, if He chooses you, if He calls you to be His collaborators, do not hesitate for a moment—following the example of the most holy Virgin to the angel—to say your generous "Yes." You will not regret it; your joy will be true and full, and your life will appear rich in fruits and in merits, because you will become with Him and for Him messengers of peace, agents of good, collaborators of God in the salvation of the world!

Pivotal Concept
of Religious Life
as Special Consecration

On May 21, 1979, His Holiness received a group of men and women Superiors General of non-Catholic religious institutes. Pope John Paul addressed them as follows:

Dearly beloved in Christ,

As Bishop of Rome I welcome you to this Apostolic See. It is especially gratifying to know that you have come for ecumenical consultation on the religious life. Your visit therefore is a propitious moment to reflect together briefly on this theme, and through this reflection to experience the joy of a common acceptance of so many great ideals of the religious life.

Among these ideals is the pivotal concept of religious life as a special consecration to our Lord Jesus Christ, as a means of adhering totally to His divine Person and of fulfilling all the exigencies of Baptism in Christ. Religious life is the radical pursuit of the beatitudes; the practical recognition of the absolute primacy of Christ in the Church and in the world. It is a free response of disciples to the invitation of the Lord Jesus: "Abide in my love" (Jn. 15:9).

The Second Vatican Council looks upon religious life as being ordered to the greater holiness of the Church and to the greater glory of the Blessed Trinity, which in Christ and through Christ is the source and origin of all holiness (cf.

Lumen gentium, no. 47). It sees all the fruitful ecclesial service of religious as resulting from intimate union with Christ (cf. *Perfectae caritatis,* no. 8).

Any consideration of religious life as a new and special title of fulfilling the universal call of all God's people to holiness brings us, moreover, of necessity to the ecclesial aspect of religious life. In the history of the Church, the ecclesiastical authority has guaranteed the authenticity of this life, and this life has constantly been viewed in its relationship to the entire Body of Christ, in which the activities of each member and of communities are advantageous to the whole Body by reason of the principle of dynamic union with Christ the Head.

Through God's grace I am confident that your ecumenical consultation on such important subjects will bring forth fruit that will last. I pray that the Holy Spirit will Himself shed light on your reflection of religious life, especially as it touches the question of Church unity—the perfect unity willed by Christ.

Who more than religious should experience in prayer the urgency, not only of manifesting unity, but also of living it in the fullness of truth and charity? And as we experience this urgency —an experience which is itself a gift of God—do we not likewise experience the need for that increased personal purification, for that ever greater conversion of heart that God seems to be requiring as a prerequisite for the restoration of the corporate unity of all Christians? And does not the spiritual freedom that religious endeavor to acquire in adhering totally to the Lord Jesus bind them ever more closely, in love, to pursue to the end the will of Christ for His Church? Are religious not called in a special way to give expression to the yearning of Christians that the ecumenical dialogue—which by its nature is temporary—should be brought to term in that full ecclesial fellowship which is "with the Father and with his Son Jesus Christ" (1 Jn. 1:3)? Should religious not be the first to pledge the fullness of their generosity before God's salvific plan, each one repeating with St. Paul: "What am I to do, Lord?" (Acts 22:10)

Dear brothers and sisters, this is a moment of joy, not founded in complacency, but in a humble and repentant desire to fulfill the will of God. It is at the same time a moment of confidence "in Christ Jesus whom God made our wisdom, our righteousness and sanctification and redemption" (1 Cor. 1:30). To Him we turn our hearts as we invoke the power of His merits to sustain us as we await, in generosity and sacrifice, the full revelation of His kingdom, the consummation of our unity in Christ: "Thy kingdom come, thy will be done."

I would ask you to take back to your religious communities my greeting and encouragement to live deeply "by faith in the Son of God" (Gal. 2:20). With the expression of my friendship and esteem I send the assurance of my love in Christ Jesus our Lord.

Missionary Nature of the Church

On the evening of May 23, 1979, His Holiness addressed the many thousands gathered in St. Peter's Square for the general audience. The following is an excerpt.

In the Church, where every one of the faithful is an evangelizer, Christ continues to choose the men He wants "that they might be with Him so that He might send them to preach to the nations" *(Ad gentes,* no. 23). In this way the story of the sending of the Apostles becomes the history of the Church from the first to the last hour.

The quality and the number of these vocations are the sign of the presence of the Holy Spirit, because it is the Spirit "who shares His gifts as He wills for the common good": for this supreme good He "implants in the hearts of individuals a missionary vocation" *(ibid.).* It is certainly the Spirit who inspires and moves the men chosen, in order that the Church can assume her evangelizing responsibility. The Church being, in fact, the mission incarnate, she reveals this incarnation of hers first of all in the men of the mission: "As the Father has sent me, even so I send you" (Jn. 20:21).

In the Church, the presence of Christ, who calls and sends us during His mortal life, and of the pentecostal Spirit, who inflames, is the certainty that missionary vocations will never be lacking.

These people "marked and designated by the Spirit" (cf. Acts 13:2) "have a special vocation, whether they are natives of the place or foreigners, priests, religious, or lay people. Having been sent by legitimate authority they go forth in faith..." (*Ad gentes,* no. 23). The arising and multiplication of people consecrated for life to the mission is also an indication of the missionary spirit of the Church: from the general missionary vocation of the Christian community there springs up the special and specific vocation of the missionary. Vocation, in fact, is never in the singular, but touches man through the community.

The Holy Spirit, who inspires the vocation of the individual, is the same who "raises up in the Church institutes that take on the duty of evangelization, which pertains to the whole Church, and make it as it were their own special task" (*ibid.*). Orders, congregations and missionary institutes have represented and lived the missionary commitment of the Church for centuries, and they still live it fully today.

The Church, therefore, confirms her trust and her mandate to these institutions, and greets with joy and hope the new ones that arise in the communities of the missionary world. But they, in their turn, being the expression of the missionary spirit also of the local Churches from which they have sprung, in which they live, and for which they operate, intend to dedicate themselves to the formation of missionaries who are the real agents of evangelization in the line of Christ's Apostles. Their number must not diminish; on the contrary, it must adapt itself to the immense necessities of the not distant times in which the peoples will open up to Christ and to His Gospel of life.

Furthermore, no one can fail to see a sign of the new missionary age which the Church is expecting and preparing. The local Churches, old and new, are vivified and shaken by a new anxiety, that of finding specifically missionary forms of action with the sending of their own members to the nations, either on their own account or cooperating with the missionary institutes. The mission of evangelization "which falls (precisely) on the whole Church" is increasingly felt as the direct commitment of the local Churches, which therefore give their priests, men and women religious and laity to the mission fields. Pope Paul VI clearly saw and described it: "An evangelizer, the Church begins by evangelizing herself.... That means, in a word, that she always needs to be evangelized if she wishes to keep freshness, élan and strength to proclaim the Gospel."

Consequently, every Church will have to put itself in the perspective of that apostolic vocation which Paul recognized himself as having among the Gentiles and because of which he groaned: "Woe to me if I do not preach the Gospel" (1 Cor. 9:16).

PRAYER CONTINUES

The first Sunday in May was dedicated particularly to prayer for vocations. We have prolonged this prayer for the whole month, commending this problem, which is so important, to Mary, Mother of Christ and of the Church.

Now in the period of the Ascension of the Lord, preparing for the solemnity of Pentecost, we wish to express in this prayer the missionary character of the Church. Therefore we also ask that the grace of missionary vocation, granted to the Church from apostolic times throughout so many centuries and so many generations, may ring out in the modern generation of Christians with a new force of faith and hope: "Go...and make disciples of all nations" (Mt. 28:19).

Religious Vocation
a Living Sign
of the "Future Century"

On June 5, 1979, Pope John Paul II celebrated Mass for women religious in the Sanctuary of Jasna Gora, and delivered the following homily.

1. Dear sisters,

I rejoice with all my heart at this meeting, disposed for us by divine Providence, today at the feet of Our Lady of Jasna Gora. You have come in such great numbers from all over Poland to participate in the pilgrimage of your fellow countryman whom Christ in His inscrutable mercy has called, as He once called Simon of Bethsaida, and commanded him to leave his native land to take upon himself the succession of the Bishops of Rome. Since he has now been given the grace to return again to these parts, he wishes to speak to you with the same words that he used in speaking to you more than once as successor of St. Stanislaus at Krakow. Those words now take on a different dimension, a universal dimension.

The theme of "religious vocation" is one of the most beautiful of which the Gospel has spoken and continues to speak to us. The theme was given a particular incarnation in Mary, who said of herself: "Behold, I am the handmaid of the Lord; let it be done to me according to your word" (Lk. 1:38). I think that these words have been echoed in the depths of the religious vocation and profession of each one of you.

2. While this opportunity to speak to you is being presented to me today, the splendid chapters of the Church's teaching in the last Council come to my mind, as do the very numerous documents of the last Popes.

I would like however, on the basis of all this wealth of teaching by the Church, to refer to some modest statements made by myself. I do so because these statements were echoes of my very numerous past meetings with religious in Poland. These meetings, as a "resource" of my personal experience, went with me to Rome. It will therefore be perhaps easier for you to find yourselves in those words, for, in spite of having been addressed in other surroundings, they speak in a way of you—of the Polish sisters and of the Polish religious families.

3. Soon after my new ministry began I had the good fortune to meet almost twenty thousand sisters from the whole of Rome. Here is a part of the talk that I gave them on that occasion:

Your "vocation is a special treasure of the Church, which can never cease to pray that the Spirit of Jesus Christ will bring forth religious vocations in souls. They are, in fact, both for the community of the People of God, and for the world, a living sign of the future life: a sign which, at the same time, is rooted (also by means of your religious habit) in the everyday life of the Church and of society, and permeates its most delicate tissues....

"(Your presence) must be a visible sign of the Gospel for all. It must also be the source of a particular apostolate. This apostolate is so varied and rich that it is even difficult for me to list here all its forms, its fields, its orientations. It is united with the specific charism of every congregation, with its apostolic spirit, which the Church and the Holy See approve with joy, seeing in it the expression of the vitality of the Mystical Body of Christ! This apostolate is usually discreet, hidden, near to the human being, and so is more suited to a woman's soul, sensitive to her neighbor, and hence called to the task of a sister and mother.

"It is precisely this vocation which is at the very 'heart' of your religious being. As Bishop of Rome I beg you: be spiritually mothers and sisters for all the people of this Church which Jesus, in His ineffable mercy and grace, has wished to entrust to me" (*L'Osservatore Romano,* November 12, 1978, p. 16).

4. On last November 24, I had the occasion to meet the large group of superiors general gathered in Rome under the leadership of the Cardinal Prefect of the Sacred Congregation for Religious and Secular Institutes. I would like to repeat some phrases from the address I gave on that occasion.

"The religious vocation...belongs to that spiritual fullness which the Spirit Himself—the Spirit of Christ—brings forth and molds in the People of God. Without religious orders, without 'consecrated' life, by means of the vows of chastity, poverty and obedience, the Church would not be fully herself.... Your houses must be, above all, centers of prayer, meditation and dialogue—personal and of the whole community—with Him who is and must remain the first and principal interlocutor in the industrious succession of your days. If you are able to nourish this 'climate' of intense and loving community with God, it will be possible for you to carry forward, without traumatic tensions or dangerous confusion, that renewal of life and discipline to which the Second Vatican Ecumenical Council committed you" (*L'Osservatore Romano,* November 25, 1978, pp. 1-2).

5. Finally, Mexico. The meeting I had in that country's capital remains indelibly inscribed in my memory and my heart. It could not be otherwise, since sisters always create in these meetings a particularly cordial atmosphere and receive with joy the words spoken to them. Here then are some thoughts from the meeting in Mexico:

"Your vocation is one that deserves the highest esteem on the part of the Pope and of the Church, today no less than yesterday. For this reason I wish to express my joyful confidence in you and to encourage you not to lose heart on the way that you have undertaken and which is worth continuing on with fresh spirit and enthusiasm.... What a lot you can do today for the Church and for humanity! They are waiting for your generous gift, the giving of your free hearts, so that your hearts may broaden their unsuspected potentialities for love in a world that is losing the capacity for altruism, for self-sacrificing and disinterested love. Remember, in fact, that you are mystical brides of Christ and of Christ crucified" (*AAS* 1979, p. 177).

Now let my thoughts and yours turn once again in this place to Our Lady of Jasna Gora, who is the source of living inspiration for each one of you. Let each one of you, as she hears the words spoken at Nazareth, repeat with Mary: "Behold, I am the handmaid of the Lord; let it be done to me according to your word" (Lk. 1:38). These words contain in a way the prototype of every religious profession, the profession by which each one of you embraces with her whole being the mystery of the grace transmitted to her in her religious vocation. Each one of you, like Mary, chooses Jesus, the divine Spouse. By fulfilling her vows of poverty, chastity and obedience, she wishes to live for Him, for love of Him. Through these vows each one of you wishes to give witness to the eternal life that Christ has brought us in His cross and resurrection.

Dear sisters, *this living sign* that each one of you constitutes in the midst of humanity is beyond price. Embracing with faith, hope and charity your divine Spouse, you embrace Him in the many people you serve: in the sick, the old, the crippled, the handicapped, people whom nobody is capable of taking care of but you because this demands a truly heroic sacrifice. Where else do you find Christ? In the children, in young people receiving catechetical instruction, in pastoral service with the priests. You will find Him in the simplest service as well as in the tasks that at times demand deep preparation and culture. You will find Him everywhere, like the bride of the Song of Solomon: "I found him whom my soul loves" (Sg. 3:4).

May Poland ever rejoice in your evangelical witness. Let there be no want of warm hearts that bring evangelical love to their neighbor. As for you, rejoice always with the joy of your vocation, even when you will have to endure inward or outward suffering or darkness.

Pope John Paul II wishes to pray with you for all this during this holy Sacrifice.

Man's Sublime Activity To Form the Human Person

On the morning of June 6, 1979, Pope John Paul II celebrated Mass at Jasna Gora for diocesan and religious seminarians and for novices. During the Mass he addressed them as follows:

My dear friends!

1. The Gospel which we often hear read when we are present here at Jasna Gora is that which recalls the wedding feast at Cana of Galilee. St. John as an eyewitness has described that event in all its particulars—an event which took place at the beginning of the public life of Christ the Lord. This is the first miracle—the first sign of the saving power of Christ—performed in the presence of His Mother and His first disciples, the future Apostles.

You also are gathered here as disciples of Christ the Lord. Each one of you has become His disciple through holy Baptism, which requires a solid preparation of our minds, our wills and our hearts. This is done by means of catechesis, first of all in our families, then in the parish. By catechesis we search ever more deeply into the mystery of Christ and we discover the meaning of our participation in it. Catechesis is not only learning religious concepts; it is an introduction to the life of participation in the mystery of Christ. Thus, knowing Christ—and through Him also the Father: "He who has seen me has seen the Father" (Jn. 14:9)—we become, in the Holy

Spirit, participants in the new life which Christ has grafted into us from the moment of Baptism and which He has strengthened with Confirmation.

2. This new life which Christ has given us becomes our spiritual life, our interior life. We therefore discover within ourselves the interior person with its qualities, talents, worthy desires and ideals; but we also discover our weaknesses, our vices, our evil inclinations: selfishness, pride and sensuality. We perfectly understand how much the first of these aspects of our humanity needs to be developed and strengthened, and how much instead the second one must be overcome, combatted and transformed. In this way—in living contact with Jesus, in the contact of the disciple with the Master—there begins and develops the most sublime activity of man: work on himself that aims at the formation of his own humanity. In our lives we prepare ourselves to perform various activities in one or another profession; our interior task, on the other hand, tends solely to form the human person himself—that human person which is each one of us.

This task is the most personal collaboration with Jesus Christ, similar to that which occurred in His disciples when He called them to intimate friendship with Him.

3. Today's Gospel speaks of a banquet. We know that the Divine Master, calling us to collaborate with Him—a collaboration which we as His disciples accept in order to become His apostles—invites us as He did at Cana of Galilee. In fact, He presents to us, as the Fathers of the

Church have described in an expressive and symbolic way, two tables: one of the Word of God, the other of the Eucharist. The work that we take on ourselves consists in approaching these two tables in order to be filled.

I know how many young people in Poland, boys and girls, who with joy, with trust, with an interior desire to know the truth and to find pure and beautiful love, approach the table of the Word of God and the table of the Eucharist. On this occasion today I wish to emphasize the great significance of the various forms of that creative work which allows us to discover the deep value of life, the true attraction of youth, living in intimacy with Christ the Master, in His sanctifying grace. One discovers in this way that human life, on whose threshold youth still finds itself, has a rich meaning and that it is—always and everywhere—a free and conscious *answer to the call of God*, a well-defined vocation.

4. Some of you have discovered that Christ has called you in a particular way to His exclusive service, and that He wishes to see you at the altar as His ministers, or on the path of evangelical consecration through the religious vows. This discovery of a vocation is followed by a particular preparation of some years either in seminaries or in religious novitiates. These institutions—worthy of praise in the life of the Church—never cease to attract young people who are ready to give themselves exclusively to the Redeemer, so that there is fulfilled what you so spontaneously sing: "Come with me to save the world, it is already the twentieth century...."

Remember that I rejoice for every priestly and religious vocation, as a particular gift of Christ the Lord for the Church, for the People of God, as a singular witness of the Christian vitality of our dioceses, parishes, families. Here, today, with you, I entrust every young vocation to Our Lady of Jasna Gora and I offer it to her as a particular gift.

5. During the banquet at Cana of Galilee, Mary asked the first sign from her Son on behalf of the young newlyweds and those in charge of the house. Mary does not cease to pray for you, for all the young people of Poland and of the whole world, so that there will be manifested in you the sign of a new presence of Christ in history.

And you, my dearest friends, remember well these words which the Mother of Christ spoke at Cana, turning to those who were to fill the water jars. She said then, pointing to her Son, "Do whatever he tells you!" (Jn. 2:5)

To you also she says the same thing today.

Accept these words.

Remember them.

Put them into practice.

Following the Example
of Jesus Christ

On June 18, 1979, the Holy Father received in audience participants in the Third National Congress of the Association of Religious Socio-medical Institutes, held from June 14 to 17, at Domus Mariae, Rome, on the subject "The Spirit calls us to give an account: testimony and service for the protection of health."

Pope John Paul II delivered the following address.

Beloved brothers and sisters!

Thanking you for your courtesy in requesting this meeting, I wish to express in the first place the deep joy that fills my heart on seeing beside me a skilled representation of the religious families operating in the socio-medical field. Looking at you, my thought goes instinctively to the vast host of generous souls who share with you the ideal of dedication to Christ and service of their brothers, and who spend their energies, like you, in the wards of hospitals or nursing homes, among persons receiving care in rehabilitation centers or among old people gathered in special institutes.

And then, as if conjured up by your presence, a multitude of other faces flash upon the inward eye: it is the world of the suffering of all ages and from all walks of life; each one with his own story, perhaps with his own bitterness, certainly with an expectation that often becomes heartbroken pleading.

Your service springs precisely from deep perception of the needs, the hopes and the disappointments felt by this portion of mankind whom the world of the healthy tends too often to forget. Your sensitiveness is inspired and prompted above all by Christ's words: "I was sick and you visited me" (Mt. 25;36). You have let yourselves be involved personally and have decided to dedicate your lives to the expectations of so many brothers. You have decided to do so in a full and complete way, renouncing everything that might have represented an obstacle to the completeness of the gift, precisely to this consecration of yours to Christ in religious life for unreserved, loving, and active availability for your neighbor's necessities.

I wish to testify to you my admiration. By your example, you continue a very noble tradition which, starting from the institution of the first deacons (cf. Acts 6:1), characterizes the whole history of the Church! I am happy to mention particularly the "hostels" of the eleventh century, frequented by pilgrims and crusaders, and the hospitals of the sixteenth century, rich in art and history. But it can be said that from the origins, up to modern medical units, there has been a whole blossoming of charitable initiatives, which draw inspiration and nourishment from the Gospel values. In this connection, it is a significant fact that, right from the most remote past, welfare structures have nearly always followed the same pattern: the cathedral and, near it, the hospital, as if with facts bearing witness to faith in the twofold presence of Christ—the real one under the eucharistic Species and the mystical one in needy or sick brothers.

It is necessary to revive awareness of these glorious traditions and of the certainties of faith that inspired them, in order to confirm in oneself faithfulness to the commitment of dedication to one's needy neighbor and the superior motivation, precisely that of faith, which enlightens and directs its accomplishment. In other words, that which even today, in an advanced society which aims at being self-sufficient, justifies the ideal that is yours, is the fact of offering the patient, together with generous and indefatigable services—not measured sometimes even by recognized rights, irreprehensible on the medical and humanitarian plane—also a living testimony of Christ's love and concern for the suffering.

Care, in fact, cannot be reduced to the strictly technico-professional aspect but must address all the elements of the human being, and therefore also his spiritual one. Now, the human spirit is by its very nature open to the religious dimension, which, in fact, is generally perceived and felt more deeply during illness and suffering. The sick person, therefore, if a Christian, will desire the presence beside him of consecrated persons who, together with all suitable technical services, are able to transcend this merely human dimension, so to speak, and, with thoughtful and patient delicacy, offer him the perspective of a vaster hope; that which was taught us by the cross, on which the Son of God was nailed for the redemption of the world. In this perspective, "every cross"—as I had the opportunity to say recently to a group of sick people during my pilgrimage in Poland—"every cross put on man's shoulders acquires a dignity that is inconceivable on the human plane, and becomes a sign of salvation for him who carries it and also for others."

Here is the deep reason that motivates your presence in the vast field of medical care: to bring to the sick, in words and by your example, a limpid and consistent testimony, which will bring to life again before their eyes some features of the lovable figure of the Savior, who "went about doing good and healing all" (Acts 10:38). Did not this command, also, ring out on Jesus' lips when He sent His disciples "to preach the kingdom of God and to heal" (Lk. 9:2; cf. 10:9)? The Church, undertaking care for the sick, merely obeys the will of service and of love of her Teacher and Lord.

Continue, with renewed enthusiasm, therefore, beloved sons and daughters, your beneficial action in the service of man. May your daily dedication be a testimony of a reality that transcends you; may Christ Himself bend with you over human suffering to relieve its torment with the balm of hope which only He can give. Be aware of this mission and live its demanding consequences consistently. It is just to help you in this commitment of yours that I would like to propose some suggestions to you.

1. The first one concerns *choice of the field of action*. In the last few years the state has made considerable progress in carrying out its medical and welfare task. In spite of this, there remain

sectors in which public care is, to a certain extent, and sometimes almost inevitably, incomplete and unsatisfactory, even today. Your interest should be directed with priority preference to these sectors.

It is obvious that, to operate well-pondered choices in this direction, it will be necessary to subject the initiatives that have matured within the individual institute to a "check" by means of an open confrontation with reality. From a community evaluation of the objective situation there may spring decisions better fitted to the real needs of the concrete social context.

2. The second suggestion concerns *the religious discourse* that goes on between you and the sick: it must aim at proposing—with respect for all, and in particular with delicacy as regards those who do not yet have the gift of faith—together with the witness of your personal life, the paschal mystery in its entirety. There is, in fact, a certain "ascesis of acceptance" which refers to a notion of "resignation" that is closer to fatalism than to Christian patience (St. Paul's *hypomoné*). In the paschal mystery, which causes the passion and death of Christ to be understood in the light of the resurrection, the Christian's vocation before illness and death is clarified: the acceptance of suffering is accompanied by the will and the commitment to do everything possible to overcome it and reduce it or surpass it for one's neighbor. In suffering, in fact, and in death is manifested the mysterious inheritance of sin, over which Christ has now triumphed definitively.

Not renunciation, therefore, before illness, but active resistance: the Christian operates to free himself from disease and death, in which, thanks to the strength that comes to him from faith in the paschal mystery, he is sustained by the certainty that life will triumph in the end.

3. I wish to entrust a last suggestion to you: it concerns *the style of your presence* beside the sick. It is a presence that has features in common with those of all persons engaged professionally in care for the sick: scientific and technical preparation, generosity of service, constant attention to the person in need of treatment. But it has also, because of the evangelical motivation that inspires it, a special feature which consists in seeing in the sick person, because of his suffering in body and in spirit, the very Person of Jesus, and which therefore can call also for sacrifice, the renunciation of rights to which you are entitled professionally and of requirements that are understandable on the human plane.

Is this not a testimony, perhaps the most important one, that you are called to give in the sphere of your work? That is, the testimony that the patient cannot but constitute a permanent priority, at the center of all medical concern and activity. And—I would like to add with great admiration and affection, because I know how much so many of you give beyond your remaining physical energies—this priority may involve, if necessary, also sacrifices on the organizational and financial plane of your institutions, especially in favor of the poorest.

As you see, yours is really not an easy task! It calls for the exercise of a charity that is modelled every day on the example of Christ who "came not to be served but to serve, and to give his life as a ransom for many" (Mt. 20:28). It is, however, in this genuinely evangelical inspiration that the nobility of your mission lies, as well as the justification of your presence in the world of the sick. The exercise of charity for brothers is a natural expression of faith, and the Church rightly claims it as a dimension of religious freedom itself, and not a marginal or a secondary one. Keep this in mind!

And in moments of weariness raise your eyes to Mary, the Virgin who, forgetting herself, set out "with haste" for the hills to reach her elderly cousin Elizabeth who was in need of help and assistance (cf. Lk. 1:39ff.). Let her be the inspiration of your daily dedication to duty; let her suggest to you the right words and opportune gestures at the bedside of the sick; let her comfort you in misunderstandings and failures, helping you always to keep a smile on your face and a hope in your heart.

With these wishes, while I confirm my esteem and affection for your association and for the institutes it represents, I embrace you all with a fatherly blessing, which I willingly extend also to the dear patients in your hospitals and to the medical and auxiliary staff, which diligently offers its competent services in them.

The Vocational Apostolate— Search, Preparation and Care

On July 6, 1979, John Paul II received in audience a group of bishops of Colombia on their visit ad limina Apostolorum. *The Holy Father, after listening to an address of homage delivered by the President of the Episcopal Conference of Colombia, His Excellency Mario Revollo, made a speech, of which the following is an excerpt.*

Among the multiple cares that concern your souls as pastors, I know there is one that has a preeminent place: the problem of priestly and religious vocations. This is, in fact, a very important subject for the whole Church, for Colombia, and in particular for your four ecclesiastical provinces. I wish to confide in you that this is one of the points to which the Pope devotes special attention, in view of the enormous repercussion it has on the general progress of the Church, for the present and for the future.

Convinced of that, I wish to give you as your personal charge what I indicated in my opening address at the Puebla Conference: that you put care for vocations among your priority pastoral tasks. It is something vital, indispensable; since a Church that lacked qualified, stable agents, completely dedicated to this ministry, could not effectively carry out the work of evangelization.

It is certain that all the members of the ecclesial community, including laity—whose help must be appreciated and expanded in every possible way—must take part, by virtue of their Christian vocation, in the evangelizing task of the

173

Church. But they cannot replace the indispensable presence of the consecrated minister or of the soul called to specific ecclesial dedication. What is more, the real maturity of the Catholic laity cannot help being reflected also in a practical opening to fully consecrated life.

THREE DIRECTIONS

In your concern for vocations you must aim in three directions: diligent search for these vocations, adequate preparation of them, and care for their perseverance. It will be opportune for this purpose to set up a well-prepared vocational apostolate which will pay careful attention to the family, the school, youth, apostolic movements; vital centers in which, if they are saturated with faith and good morals, there germinate so many decisions of commitment to the service of God and one's neighbor.

Do not, therefore, consider it superfluous or less productive on the apostolic plane to dedicate to this work well-qualified priests of great spirit, who attend preferably to this sector, in the framework of some good diocesan and even national plans to which I know you give careful attention. And, in that, interest all priests, men and women religious, and committed laity.

HOUSES OF FORMATION

You should give no less care to seminaries and houses of religious formation which—as indicated on various occasions, also recently, by the Holy See—must always be a center for the preparation of well-balanced human personalities, with all the healthy opening that the present moment requires, with a solid spiritual, moral, and intellectual basis, capable of disciplined life and the spirit of sacrifice. Without that, the interior structure of a vocation for the Church and the world of today cannot be constructed. A fundamental premise must never be forgotten: if we present debased values, the young people themselves are the first to reject them, since they do not discover in them a framework in which to pour all their generosity and longing for dedication.

Do not fail either to give due care to the apostolate of adult vocations, which in certain environments and also in Colombia are a more and more frequent and promising phenomenon.

BROTHERLY SERVICE

Finally, take to heart diligently the perseverance of those who are already living complete consecration. Do not fear to spend your time and best energies in this task. In the line indicated in my recent Letter to the Bishops, on the occasion of Holy Thursday, above all, be real friends and supporters, with your work and your luminous example, of priests and consecrated souls. May your life and effort be a precious help, in the spirit of brotherly service, to maintain in them clear awareness of their own identity as the chosen.

Beloved brothers: here are some guidelines for you, to be completed with your zeal and creativity as pastors.

Let my last word be a brotherly call to hope and to prayer to the Lord of the harvest, not to abandon us. May He make your efforts fruitful. May Mary, our Mother, accompany you always. My prayer for you and for each member of your ecclesial communities accompanies you, while I bless you all with special affection.

Your Hidden Sacrifices Help To Build Up the Church

On September 3, 1979, Pope John Paul II went to the Hospital of the Daughters of St. Paul, Regina Apostorum, in Albano. He celebrated Holy Mass in the chapel and then visited the various wards. The Pope delivered the following homily.

Here I am in your midst, beloved sisters, for whom illness reserves, with its hard ordeals, closer union with the suffering Christ. I greet you with fatherly affection, I thank you for the invitation addressed to me, and above all, for all that you are able to suffer and offer for the salvation of so many souls.

1. "Today this scripture has been fulfilled in your hearing" (Lk. 4:21).

With these words the Lord Jesus at the Synagogue of Nazareth *fulfills* and *actualizes* the Scriptures and the salvation contained in them.

Also St. Paul's exhortation to the inhabitants of Thessalonica, which we heard in the first reading of this sacred Liturgy, urges us to consider the time of hope, not like the pagans who do not have this consolation (1 Thes. 4:13), but as the temple of God, the today of God, that is, the "short time" (cf. 1 Cor. 7:29) reserved for us to bring about salvation.

This salvation does not lie in an abstract reality or a philosophical system, but it is a Person: it is Jesus Himself, who was sent by the Father to accomplish the work of liberation of all those who, according to the passage of the prophet

Isaiah now proclaimed in the Gospel (cf. Lk. 4:18-19 and Is. 61:1-2), are "poor," "oppressed," "captives" and "sick," going through trials and rejections in his own country and outside it for this purpose, and facing the passion and death.

LISTENING AND ACCEPTING

2. The privileged time of God is above all that in which we listen to, and accept with faith, the divine word, which "is piercing to the spirit...and discerning the thoughts and intentions of the heart" (Heb. 4:12) and therefore becomes incarnate in us. But it is also the time that is realized in the sacramental sign, and above all in the Eucharist, which we are preparing to celebrate together at this holy Mass, in which God's time is given its rhythm by the inseparable dual concept of death and the resurrection. In the Eucharistic Sacrifice, in fact, there is accomplished in us, in an admirable way, the salvific event, the time of salvation, which involves completely both the individual life and the community life of us all. In it a personal conversion takes place by means of union with Christ the Victim, and at the same time a community conversion, expressed in the exchange of forgiveness and peace among those present.

In this connection, St. Gregory the Great, my venerated predecessor, whose memory we celebrate today, defines very well, in some famous texts, these two moments which are realized in the Eucharistic Sacrifice. The great Doctor of the Church states: "Christ will really be for us a host of reconciliation with God, if we strive to become hosts ourselves," and with regard to the community dimension, which, in holy Mass, makes us ask for and grant forgiveness and reconciles us with our brothers, he says: "God does not receive our offer, unless discord is first dispelled from our hearts" (cf. *Dialogues*, chapters 58 and 60).

3. Here, beloved sisters, are some simple thoughts on the times and ways of salvation, offered to us by reading the biblical passages of this Mass. Continue to commit yourselves for a more and more conscious realization of these great themes of your faith. At moments when you may feel human weakness, which accompanies illness, remember the marvelous experience of St. Paul, who, afflicted by his "thorn in the flesh," was comforted by the Lord with these words: "My grace is sufficient for you, for my power is made perfect in weakness" (2 Cor. 12:9).

AIDING THE CHURCH

On my side, I assure you that, if I rely greatly on the spiritual aid of all the sick, I count all the more on you, on your prayers, on the value of your sufferings, because you join to the charism of the vocation of a life entirely consecrated to God the incomparable riches of your infirmity, so that each of you can really say: *Adimpleo.* I ask you, therefore: continue to help the Church in this way, to build it up with your hidden sacrifices, with your mysterious and painful cooperation. Continue to help mankind, in order to reach that interior health which is synonymous with serenity and peace of soul, without which physical health and all other earthly boons would be of no avail.

May you be assisted in this common effort by the Blessed Virgin, invoked by you under the title of "Queen of Apostles," and may there always hover over you the blessed spirit of your venerated Founder, Don Giacomo Alberione, from whose apostolic heart there sprang this providential nursing home and place of Christian assistance. Amen!

Be Authentic Imitators
of Our Lady

*During his pilgrimage to Loreto on September 8, 1979,
the Holy Father met the bishops, clergy and the male
and female religious of the Marches. The meeting took
place in the Basilica of the Holy House, and Pope John
Paul II addressed them as follows:*

I am very grateful to Monsignor Marcello
Morgante, Bishop of Ascoli Piceno and President
of the Bishops' Conference of the Marche Region,
for his kind words of homage, in which he well
summed up the feelings of all at this meeting, in
this place and time.

I very much wished, dear brothers and sisters in Christ, to have a warm meeting with you
on this memorable day. You merit this because
you are people consecrated to God: belonging
to families and religious institutes of men and
women; you are called, through your holy vows,
to the state of perfection.

Your sentiments of fidelity to Christ and the
Church I see eloquently expressed more by your
eyes, the pledge and reflection of the interior
light of your souls enriched by so many spiritual
gifts, than by the manifestation of joy with which
you welcomed me. It seems to me that I could put
to you this question: how could we respond better
to the expectations of the whole People of God,
especially in the grave difficulties of the present
hour? In this Marian city I think I could reply: by
being authentic imitators of our Lady.

Like her, may you know how to keep all these things in your heart (cf. Lk. 2:32) which the Redeemer will suggest to you when you seek Him with joy, perseverance, and trepidation.

Let your mission to your neighbor be like that of Mary, in eager love serving her relation, Elizabeth. Let your mission be full of God through the grace that activates and guides it, solicitous through the love that characterizes it, disinterested because it seeks no human recompense, discrete because of the intimacy of the message it must carry.

As the Virgin shared little in the few triumphs of her Son, but was very near to Him when He hung on the cross, so you too, not looking for the ephemeral satisfactions of the earth but thinking of human sufferings, must know how to accept with ineffable dedication the extreme consequences of the spiritual fatherhood or motherhood of those whom Christ has entrusted to you, and of the whole human race, which has need of your example and witness.

These are the prospects which, in the name of the holy Virgin, I feel it my duty and my joy to leave you here near the house of humility, love, obedience.

While I insistently ask for your prayers, I promise you that you will always be accompanied by a remembrance in my prayers and by my blessing, which I extend to all those dear to you.

What the People Expect of You Is Fidelity

To the vast gathering of priests, religious men and women, missionaries and seminarians in St. Patrick's College in Maynooth, near Dublin, on October 1, 1979, the Holy Father delivered the following address.

My dear brothers and sisters in Christ,

1. The name of Maynooth is respected all over the Catholic world. It recalls what is noblest in the Catholic priesthood in Ireland. Here come seminarians from every Irish diocese, sons of Catholic homes which were themselves true "seminaries," true seedbeds of priestly or religious vocations. From here have gone out priests to every Irish diocese and to the dioceses of the far-flung Irish diaspora. Maynooth has, in this century, given birth to two new missionary societies, one initially directed towards China, the other towards Africa; and it has sent out hundreds of alumni as volunteers to the mission fields. Maynooth is a school of priestly holiness, an academy of theological learning, a university of Catholic inspiration. St. Patrick's College is a place of rich achievement, which promises a future just as great.

Therefore Maynooth is a fitting place in which to meet and talk with priests, diocesan and religious, with religious brothers, religious sisters, missionaries and seminarians. Having, as a priest-student in Paris, lived for a time in the atmosphere of the Irish Seminary—the College Irlandais in Paris, now loaned by the Irish bishops to the hierarchy of Poland—I have profound joy in meeting with you all here in Ireland's National Seminary.

2. My first words go to the priests, diocesan and religious. I say to you what St. Paul said to Timothy. I ask you "to fan into a flame the gift that God gave you when (the bishop) laid (his) hands on you" (2 Tm. 1:6). Jesus Christ Himself, the one High Priest, said: "I have come to bring fire to the earth, and how I wish it were blazing already!" (Lk. 12:49) You share in His priesthood; you carry on His work in the world. His work cannot be done by lukewarm or half-hearted priests. His fire of love for the Father and for men must burn in you. His longing to save mankind must consume you.

You are called by Christ as the Apostles were. You are appointed, like them, to be with Christ. You are sent, as they were, to go out in His name, and by His authority to "make disciples of all the nations" (cf. Mt. 10:1, 28:29; Mk. 3:13-16).

Your first duty is to be *with Christ.* You are each called to be "a witness to his resurrection" (Acts 1:22). A constant danger with priests, even zealous priests, is that they become so immersed in the work of the Lord that they neglect the Lord of the work.

We must find time, we must make time, to be with the Lord in prayer. Following the example of the Lord Jesus Himself, we must "always go off to some place where [we can] be alone and pray" (cf. Lk. 5:16). It is only if we spend time with the Lord that our sending out to others will be also a bringing of Him to others.

3. To be with the Lord is always also to be sent by Him to do His work. A priest is *called* by Christ; a priest is *with* Christ; a priest is *sent* by Christ. A priest is sent in the power of the same Holy Spirit which drove Jesus untiringly along the roads of life, the roads of history. Whatever the difficulties, the disappointments, the setbacks, we priests find in Christ and in the power of His Spirit the strength to "struggle wearily on, helped only by his power driving [us] irresistibly" (cf. Col. 1:29).

As priests, you are privileged to be pastors of a faithful people, who continue to respond generously to your ministry, and who are a strong support to your own priestly vocation through their faith and their prayer. If you keep striving to be the kind of priest your people expect and wish you to be, then you will be holy priests. The degree of religious practice in Ireland is high. For this we must be constantly thanking God. But will this high level of religious practice continue? Will the next generation of young Irishmen and Irishwomen still be as faithful as their fathers were? After my two days in Ireland, after my meeting with Ireland's youth in Galway, I am confident that they will. But this will require both unremitting work and untiring prayer on your part. You must work for the Lord with a sense of urgency. You must work with the conviction that this generation, this decade of the 1980's which we are about to enter, could be crucial and decisive for the future of the Faith in Ireland. Let there be no complacency. As St. Paul said: "Be aware of all the dangers; stay firm in the faith; be brave and be strong" (1 Cor. 16:13). Work with confidence, work with joy. We are witnesses to the Resurrection of Christ.

4. What the people expect from you, more than anything else, is faithfulness to the priesthood. This is what speaks to them of the faithfulness of God. This is what strengthens them to be faithful to Christ through all the difficulties of their lives, of their marriages. In a world so marked by instability as our world today, we need more signs and witnesses to God's fidelity to us, and to the fidelity we owe to Him. This is what causes such great sadness to the Church, such great but often silent anguish among the People of God: when priests fail in their fidelity to their priestly commitment. That counter-sign, that counter-witness, has been one of the setbacks to the great hopes for renewal aroused throughout the Church by the Second Vatican Council. Yet this has also driven priests, and the whole Church, to more intense and fervent prayer; for it has taught us all that without Christ we can do nothing (cf. Jn. 15:5). And the fidelity of the immense majority of priests has shone with even greater clarity and is all the more manifest and glorious a witness to the faithful God, and to Christ, the faithful Witness (cf. Rv. 1:5).

5. In a center of theological learning, which is also a seminary, like Maynooth, this witness of fidelity has the added importance and the special

value of impressing on candidates for the priesthood the strength and the grandeur of priestly fidelity. Here in Maynooth, theological learning, being part of formation for the priesthood, is preserved from ever being an academic pursuit of the intellect only. Here theological scholarship is linked with liturgy, with prayer, with the building of a community of faith and love, and thus with the building up, the "edifying," of the priesthood of Ireland, and the edifying of the Church. My call today is a call to prayer. Only in prayer will we meet the challenges of our ministry and fulfill the hopes of tomorrow. All our appeals for peace and reconciliation can be effective only through prayer.

This theological learning, here as everywhere throughout the Church, is a reflection on faith, a reflection in faith. A theology which did not deepen faith and lead to prayer might be a discourse on words about God; it could not be a discourse about God, the living God, the God who *is* and whose being is *Love*. It follows that theology can only be authentic in the Church, the community of faith. Only when the teaching of theologians is in conformity with the teaching of the college of bishops, united with the Pope, can the People of God know with certitude that that teaching is "the faith which has been once and for all entrusted to the saints" (Jude 3). This is not a limitation for theologians, but a liberation; for it preserves them from subservience to changing fashions and binds them securely to the unchanging truth of Christ, the truth which makes us free (Jn. 7:32).

6. In Maynooth, in Ireland, to speak of priesthood is to speak of mission. Ireland has never forgotten that "the pilgrim Church is missionary by her very nature; for it is from the mission of the Son and the mission of the Holy Spirit that she takes her origin, in accordance with the decree of God the Father" *(Ad gentes,* no. 2). In the ninth and tenth centuries, Irish monks rekindled the light of faith in regions where it had burnt low or been extinguished by the collapse of the Roman Empire, and evangelized new nations not yet evangelized, including areas of my own native Poland. How can I forget that there was an Irish monastery as far east as Kiev, even up to the thirteenth century; and that there was even an Irish college for a short time in my own city of Krakow, during the persecution of Cromwell? In the eighteenth and nineteenth centuries, Irish priests followed their exiles all over the English-speaking world. In the twentieth century, new missionary institutes of men and women sprang up in Ireland, which, altogether with the Irish branches of international missionary institutes and with existing Irish religious congregations, gave a new missionary impetus to the Church.

May that missionary spirit never decline in the hearts of Irish priests, whether members of missionary institutes or of the diocesan clergy or of religious congregations devoted to other apostolates. May this spirit be actively fostered by all of you among the laity, already so devoted in their prayer, so generous in their support for the missions. May a spirit of partnership grow between the home dioceses and the home religious congregations in the total mission of the Church, until each local diocesan Church and each religious congregation and community is fully seen to be "missionary of its very nature," entering into the eager missionary movement of the universal Church.

I have learned with pleasure that the Irish Missionary Union plans to establish a National Missionary Center, which will both serve as a focus for missionary renewal by missionaries themselves and foster the missionary awareness of the clergy, religious and faithful of the Irish Church. May its work be blessed by God. May it contribute to a great new upsurge of missionary fervor and a new wave of missionary vocations from this great motherland of faith which is Ireland.

7. I wish to speak a special word to religious brothers. The past decade has brought great changes, and with them problems and trials unprecedented in all your previous experience. I ask you not to be discouraged. Be men of great truth, of great and unbounded hope. "May the God of hope bring you such joy and peace in your faith that the power of the Holy Spirit will remove all bounds to hope" (Rom. 15:13). The past decade has also brought a great renewal in your understanding of your holy vocation, a great deepening of your liturgical lives and your prayer, a great extension of the field of your apostolic influence. I ask God to bless you with renewed fidelity in vocation among your members, and with increased vocations to your institutes. The Church in Ireland and in the missions

owes much to all the institutes of brothers. Your call to holiness is a precious adornment of the Church. Believe in your vocation. Be faithful to it. "God has called you and he will not fail you" (1 Thes. 5:23).

8. The sisters, too, have known years of searching, sometimes perhaps of uncertainty or of unrest. These have also been years of purification. I pray that we are now entering a period of consolidation and of construction. Many of you are engaged in the apostolate of education and the pastoral care of youth. Do not doubt the continuing relevance of that apostolate, particularly in modern Ireland, where youth are such a large and important part of the population. The Church has repeatedly, in many solemn recent documents, reminded religious of the primary importance of education, and has invited congregations of men and women with the tradition and the charism of education to persevere in that vocation and to redouble their commitment to it. The same is true of the traditional apostolates of care of the sick, nursing, care of the aged, the handicapped, the poor. These must not be neglected while new apostolates are being undertaken. In the words of the Gospel, you must "bring out from (your) storeroom things both new and old" (cf. Mt. 13:52). You must be courageous in your apostolic undertakings, not letting difficulties, shortage of personnel, insecurity for the future, deter or depress you.

But remember always that your field of apostolate is your own personal lives. Here is where the message of the Gospel has first to be preached and lived. Your first apostolic duty is your own sanctification. No change in religious life has any importance unless it be also conversion of yourselves to Christ. No movement in religious life has any importance unless it be also movement inwards to the "still center" of your existence, where Christ is. It is not what you *do* that matters most; but what you *are,* as women consecrated to God. For you, Christ has consecrated Himself, so that you too "may be consecrated in truth" (cf. Jn. 17:19).

9. To you and to priests, diocesan and religious, I say: rejoice to be witnesses to Christ in the modern world. Do not hesitate to be recognizable, identifiable, in the streets as men and women who have consecrated their lives to God and who have given up everything worldly to follow Christ. Believe that contemporary men and women set value on the visible signs of the consecration of your lives. People need signs and reminders of God in the modern secular city, which has few reminders of God left. Do not help the trend towards "taking God off the streets" by adopting secular modes of dress and behavior yourselves!

10. My special blessing and greeting goes to the cloistered sisters and contemplatives, men as well as women. I express to you my gratitude for what you have done for me by your lives of prayer and sacrifice since my papal ministry began. I express the Pope's need for you, the Church's need for you. You are foremost in that "great, intense and growing prayer" for which I called in *Redemptor hominis.* Never was the

contemplative vocation more precious or more relevant than in our modern restless world. May there be many Irish boys and girls called to the contemplative life, at this time when the future of the Church and the future of humanity depends on prayer.

Gladly do I repeat to all contemplatives, on this feast of St. Theresa of Lisieux, the words I used in addressing the sisters of Rome: "I commend to you the Church; I commend mankind and the world to you. To you, to your prayers, to your 'holocaust' I commend also myself, Bishop of Rome. Be with me, close to me, you who are in the heart of the Church! May there be fulfilled in each of you that which was the program of life for St. Theresa of the Child Jesus: *in corde Ecclesiae amor ero*—'I will be love in the heart of the Church'!"

Much of what I have been saying has been intended also for the seminarians. You are preparing for the total giving of yourselves to Christ and to service of His kingdom. You bring to Christ the gift of your youthful enthusiasm and vitality. In you Christ is eternally youthful; and through you He gives youth to the Church. Do not disappoint Him. Do not disappoint the people who are waiting for you to bring Christ to them. Do not fail your generation of young Irish men and women. Bring Christ to the young people of your generation as the only answer to their longings. Christ looks on you and loves you. Do not, like the young man in the Gospel, go away sad, "because he had great possessions" (cf. Mt. 19:22). Instead, bring all your possessions of mind and hand and heart to Christ, that He may use them to "draw all men to himself" (cf. Jn. 12:32).

To all of you I say: this is a wonderful time in the history of the Church. This is a wonderful time to be a priest, to be a religious, to be a missionary for Christ. Rejoice in the Lord always. Rejoice in your vocation. I repeat to you the words of St. Paul: "I want you to be happy, always happy in the Lord; I repeat, what I want is your happiness. There is no need to worry; but if there is anything you need, pray for it, asking God for it with prayer and thanksgiving, and that peace of God, which is so much greater than we can understand, will guard your hearts and your thoughts, in Christ Jesus" (Phil. 4:4-7).

Mary, Mother of Christ, the eternal Priest, Mother of priests and of religious, will keep you from all anxiety, as you "wait in joyful hope for the coming of our Lord and Savior, Jesus Christ." Entrust yourselves to her, as I commend you to her, to Mary, Mother of Jesus and Mother of His Church.

Dedication to Christ
and His Word

The Holy Father met the seminarians on October 1, 1979, in the Chapel of St. Patrick's College at Maynooth. The following is the text of the address.

Dear brothers and sons in our Lord Jesus Christ,

You have a very special place in my heart and in the heart of the Church. During my visit to Maynooth I wanted to be alone with you, even though it could be for only a few moments.

I have many things that I would tell you—things that I have been saying about the life of seminarians and about seminaries all during the first year of my pontificate.

In particular I would like to speak again about the Word of God: about how you are called to hear and guard and do the Word of God. And about how you are to base your entire lives and ministry upon the Word of God, just as it is transmitted by the Church, just as it is expounded by the magisterium, just as it has been understood throughout the history of the Church by the faithful guided by the Holy Spirit: *semper et ubique et ab omnibus.* The Word of God is the great treasure of your lives. Through the Word of God you will come to a deep knowledge of the mystery of Jesus Christ, Son of God and Son of Mary: Jesus Christ, the High Priest of the New Testament and the Savior of the world.

The Word of God is worthy of all your efforts. To embrace it in its purity and integrity, and to spread it by word and example is a great mission. And this is your mission, today and tomorrow and for the rest of your lives.

As you pursue your vocation—a vocation so intimately related to the Word of God, I wish to recall to you one simple but important lesson taken from the life of St. Patrick, and it is this: in the history of evangelization, the destiny of an entire people—your people—was radically affected for time and eternity because of the fidelity with which St. Patrick embraced and proclaimed the Word of God, and by reason of the fidelity with which St. Patrick pursued his call to the end.

What I really want you to realize is this: that God counts on you: that He makes His plans, in a way, depend on your free collaboration, on the oblation of your lives, and on the generosity with which you follow the inspirations of the Holy Spirit in the depths of your hearts.

The Catholic Faith of Ireland today was linked, in God's plan, to the fidelity of St. Patrick. And tomorrow, yes, tomorrow some part of God's plan will be linked to your fidelity—to the fervor with which you say "yes" to God's Word in your lives.

Today Jesus Christ is making this appeal to you through me: the appeal for fidelity. In prayer you will see more and more every day what I mean and what the implications of this call are. By God's grace you will understand more and more every day how God requires and accepts your fidelity as a condition for the supernatural effectiveness of all your activity. The supreme expression of fidelity will come with your irre-vocable and total self-giving in union with Jesus Christ to His Father. And may our blessed Mother Mary help you to make this gift acceptable.

Remember St. Patrick. Remember what the fidelity of just one man has meant for Ireland and the world. Yes, dear sons and brothers, fidelity to Jesus Christ and to His Word makes all the difference in the world. Let us therefore look up to Jesus, who is for all time the faithful Witness of the Father.

"You Witness to the Love of Christ"

A crowd estimated at two million lined the route along which passed the cortege of cars that accompanied the Holy Father from the airport into the city of Boston on October 1, 1979. Stopping at the Cathedral of Holy Cross, the Holy Father met the diocesan and religious clergy, and the religious women of the Archdiocese of Boston and other dioceses of New England. The assembly of more than two thousand persons was led by Cardinal Humberto Medeiros, who delivered an address of welcome. After a brief Liturgy of the Word, Pope John Paul spoke to the group. The following is an excerpt.

I wish to extend a special blessing to you religious, both religious brothers and sisters, who have consecrated your lives to Jesus Christ. May you always find joy in His love. And to all of you, the laity of this diocese, who are united with the Cardinal and the clergy in a common mission, I open my heart in love and trust. You are the workers for evangelization in the realities of daily life, and you give witness to the love of Christ in the service that you give to all your fellow men and women, beginning with your own families.

Who Will Separate Us from Christ?

In the course of morning prayer in St. Patrick's Cathedral, on October 3, 1979, in the presence of numerous bishops, priests, religious, seminarians, laity and guests of other Christian faiths, Pope John Paul II gave the following brief address.

Dear brothers and sisters,

St. Paul asks: "Who will separate us from the love of Christ?"

As long as we remain what we are this morning—a community of prayer united in Christ, an ecclesial community of praise and worship of the Father—we shall understand and experience the answer: that no one—nothing at all—will ever separate us from the love of Christ. For us today, the Church's morning prayer is a joyful, communal celebration of God's love in Christ.

The value of the Liturgy of the Hours is enormous. Through it, all the faithful, but especially the clergy and religious, fulfill a role of prime importance: Christ's prayer goes on in the world. The Holy Spirit Himself intercedes for God's people (cf. Rom. 8:27). The Christian community, with praise and thanksgiving, glorifies the wisdom, the power, the providence and the salvation of our God.

In this prayer of praise we lift up our hearts to the Father of our Lord Jesus Christ, bringing with us the anguish and hopes, the joys and sorrows of all our brothers and sisters in the world.

And our prayer becomes likewise a school of sensitivity, making us aware of how much our destinies are linked together in the human family. Our prayer becomes a school of love—a special kind of Christian consecrated love, by which we love the world, but with the heart of Christ.

Through this prayer of Christ to which we give voice, our day is sanctified, our activities transformed, our actions are made holy. We pray the same psalms that Jesus prayed, and come into personal contact with Him—the Person to whom all Scripture points, the goal to which all history is directed.

In our celebration of the Word of God, the mystery of Christ opens up before us and envelops us. And through union with our Head, Jesus Christ, we become ever more increasingly one with all the members of His Body. As never before, it becomes possible for us to reach out and embrace the world, but to embrace it with Christ: with authentic generosity, with pure and effective love, in service, in healing and reconciliation.

The efficacy of our prayer renders special honor to the Father because it is made always through Christ, and for the glory of His name: "We ask this through our Lord Jesus Christ, your Son, who lives and reigns with you and the Holy Spirit, one God, for ever and ever."

As a community of prayer and praise, with the Liturgy of the Hours among the highest priorities of our day—each day—we can be sure that nothing will separate us from the love of God that is in Christ Jesus our Lord.

The Heritage of
St. Francis of Assisi

After his meeting with the clergy and faithful of the Archdiocese of Chicago at Holy Name Cathedral, Pope John Paul, on October 4, 1979, went to the Church of St. Peter where hundreds of religious had gathered. During the prayer meeting which concluded the Pope's first day in Chicago His Holiness delivered the following address.

Brothers in Christ,

1. "I thank my God whenever I think of you; and every time I pray for you, I pray with joy, remembering how you have helped to spread the good news from the day you first heard it right up to the present" (Phil. 1:3-5). These words of St. Paul express my feelings this evening. It is good to be with you. And I am grateful to God for your presence in the Church and for your collaboration in proclaiming the Good News.

Brothers, Christ is the purpose and the measure of our lives. In the knowledge of Christ, your vocation took its origin; and in His love, your life is sustained. For He has called you to follow Him more closely in a life consecrated through the gift of the evangelical counsels. You follow Him in sacrifice and willing generosity. You follow Him in joy, "singing gratefully to God from your hearts in psalms, hymns, and inspired songs" (Col. 3:16). And you follow Him in fidelity, even considering it an honor to suffer humiliation for the sake of His name (cf. Acts 5:42).

Your religious consecration is essentially an act of love. It is an imitation of Christ who gave Himself to His Father for the salvation of the world. In Christ, the love of His Father and His love for mankind are united. And so it is with you. Your religious consecration has not only deepened your baptismal gift of union with the Trinity, but it has also called you to greater service of the People of God. You are united more closely to the Person of Christ, and you share more fully in His mission for the salvation of the world.

It is about your share in the mission of Christ that I wish to speak this evening.

FREE INTERIORLY

2. Let me begin by reminding you of the personal qualities needed to share effectively with Christ in His mission. In the first place, you must be interiorly free, spiritually free. The freedom of which I speak is a paradox to many; it is even misunderstood by some who are members of the Church. Nevertheless it is the fundamental human freedom, and it was won for us by Christ on the cross. As St. Paul said, "We were still helpless when at his appointed moment Christ died for sinful men" (Rom. 5:6).

This spiritual freedom which you received in Baptism you have sought to increase and strengthen through your willing acceptance of the call to follow Jesus more closely in poverty, chastity and obedience. No matter what others may contend or the world may believe, your promises to observe the evangelical counsels have not shackled your freedom: you are not less free because you are obedient; and you are not less loving because of your celibacy. On the contrary, the faithful practice of the evangelical counsels accentuates your human dignity, liberates the human heart and causes your spirit to burn with undivided love for Christ and for His brothers and sisters in the world (cf. *Perfectae caritatis,* nos. 1, 12).

But this freedom of an undivided heart (cf. 1 Cor. 7:32-35) must be maintained by continual vigilance and fervent prayer. If you unite yourself continually to Christ in prayer, you shall always be free and ever more eager to share in His mission.

EUCHARIST-CENTERED

3. Secondly, you must center your life around the Eucharist. While you share in many ways in the passion, death and resurrection of Christ, it is especially in the Eucharist where this is celebrated and made effective. At the Eucharist, your spirit is renewed, your mind and heart are refreshed and you will find the strength to live day by day for Him who is the Redeemer of the world.

GOD'S WORD

4. Thirdly, be dedicated to God's Word. Remember the words of Jesus: "My mother and my brothers are those who hear the word of God and put it into practice" (Lk. 8:21). If you sincerely listen to God's Word, and humbly but per-

sistently try to put it into practice, like the seed sown in fertile soil, His Word will bear fruit in your life.

FRATERNAL LIFE

5. The fourth and final element which makes effective your sharing in Christ's mission is fraternal life. Your life lived in religious community is the first concrete expression of love of neighbor. It is there that the first demands of self-sacrifice and generous service are exercised in order to build up the fraternal community. This love which unites you as brothers in community becomes in turn the force which supports you in your mission for the Church.

SEEK HOLINESS

6. Brothers in Christ, today the universal Church honors St. Francis of Assisi. As I think of this great saint, I am reminded of his delight in God's creation, his childlike simplicity, his poetic marriage to "Lady Poverty," his missionary zeal and his desire to share fully in the cross of Christ. What a splendid heritage he has handed on to those among you who are Franciscans, and to all of us.

Similarly, God has raised up many other men and women outstanding in holiness. These, too, He destined to found religious families which, each in a distinctive way, would play an important role in the mission of the Church. The key to the effectiveness of every one of these religious institutes has been their faithfulness to the original charism God had begun in their founder or foundress for the enrichment of the Church. For this reason, I repeat the words of Paul VI: "Be faithful to the spirit of your founders, to their evangelical intentions and to the example of their holiness.... It is precisely here that the dynamism proper to each religious family finds its origin" (*Evangelica testificatio*, nos. 11-12). And this remains a secure basis for judging what specific ecclesial activities each institute, and every individual member, should undertake in order to fulfill the mission of Christ.

7. Never forget the specific and ultimate aim of all apostolic service: to lead the men and women of our day to communion with the most holy Trinity. In the present age, mankind is increasingly tempted to seek security in possessions, knowledge and power. By the witness of your life consecrated to Christ in poverty, chastity and obedience, you challenge this false security. You are a living reminder that Christ alone is "the way, the truth and the life" (Jn. 14:6).

ACTIVE APOSTOLATE

8. Religious brothers today are involved in a wide range of activities: teaching in Catholic schools, spreading God's Word in missionary activity, responding to a variety of human needs by both your witness and your actions, and serving by prayer and sacrifice. As you go forward in your particular service, keep in mind the advice of St. Paul: "Whatever you do, work at it with your whole being. Do it for the Lord rather than

for men" (Col. 3:23). For the measure of your effectiveness will be the degree of your love for Jesus Christ.

9. Finally, every form of apostolic service, of either an individual or a community, must be in accord with the Gospel as it is put forward by the magisterium. For all Christian service is aimed at spreading the Gospel; and all Christian service incorporates Gospel values. Therefore be men of God's Word: men whose hearts burn within them when they hear the Word proclaimed (cf. Lk. 24:32); who shape every action according to its demands; and who desire to see the Good News proclaimed to the ends of the earth.

Brothers, your presence in the Church and your collaboration in promoting the Gospel are an encouragement and joy to me in my role as Pastor of the whole Church. May God give each of you long life. May He call many others to follow Christ in the religious life. And may the Virgin Mary, Mother of the Church and model of consecrated life, obtain for you the joy and consolation of Christ, her Son.

Mary, Sign of Hope
for All Generations

In the Church of the Immaculate Conception at the National Shrine, Pope John Paul addressed the large gathering of religious women on the morning of October 7, 1979. The Holy Father invited the religious to look on Mary as their model; he spoke as follows:

My first desire, in this National Shrine of the Immaculate Conception, is to direct my thoughts, to turn my heart to the woman of salvation history. In the eternal design of God, this woman, Mary, was chosen to enter into the work of the Incarnation and Redemption. This design of God was to be actuated through her free decision given in obedience to the divine will. Through her "yes," a "yes" that pervades and is reflected in all history, she consented to be the Virgin Mother of our saving God, the handmaid of the Lord, and at the same time the Mother of all the faithful who in the course of the centuries would become brothers and sisters of her Son. Through her, the Sun of justice was to rise in the world. Through her the great Healer of humanity, the reconciler of hearts and consciences, her Son, the God-Man, Jesus Christ, was to transform the human condition and by His death and resurrection uplift the entire human family. As a great sign that appeared in the heavens, in the fullness of time, the woman dominates all history as the Virgin Mother of the Son and as the spouse of the Holy Spirit, as the handmaid of humanity.

The woman becomes also, by association with her Son, the sign of contradiction to the world, and at the same time the sign of hope, whom all generations shall call blessed. The woman who conceived spiritually before she conceived physically, the woman who accepted the Word of God, the woman who was inserted intimately and irrevocably into the mystery of the Church, exercising a spiritual motherhood with regard to all peoples. The woman who is honored as Queen of Apostles, without herself being inserted into the hierarchical constitution of the Church, and yet this woman made all hierarchy possible because she gave to the world the Shepherd and Bishop of our souls. This woman, this Mary of the Gospels, who is not mentioned as being at the Last Supper, comes back again at the foot of the cross, in order to consummate her contribution to salvation history. By her courageous act she prefigures and anticipates the courage of all women throughout the ages who concur in bringing forth Christ in every generation.

At Pentecost, the Virgin Mother once again comes forward to exercise her role in union with the Apostles, with and in and over the Church. Yet again, she conceived of the Holy Spirit to bring forth Jesus in the fullness of His Body, the Church, never to leave Him, never to abandon Him, but to continue to love and to cherish Him through the ages.

This is the woman of history and destiny who inspires us today, the woman who speaks to us of femininity, human dignity and love, and who is the greatest expression of total consecration to Jesus Christ, in whose name we are gathered today.

Without Love Religious Life Is Incomprehensible

After his words upholding the dignity of the Blessed Virgin as model for religious, October 7, 1979, the Holy Father went on to speak to all the religious gathered in the Shrine of the Immaculate Conception as follows:

Dear sisters,

May the grace, love and peace of God our Father and our Lord Jesus Christ be with you.

I welcome this opportunity to speak with you today. I am happy for this occasion because of my esteem for religious life, and my gratitude to women religious for their invaluable contribution to the mission and very life of the Church.

I am especially pleased that we are gathered here in the National Shrine of the Immaculate Conception, for the Virgin Mary is the model of the Church, the Mother of the faithful and the perfect example of consecrated life.

1. On the day of our Baptism, we received the greatest gift God can bestow on any man or woman. No other honor, no other distinction will equal its value. For we were freed from sin and incorporated into Christ Jesus and His Body, the Church. That day and every day after, we were chosen "to live through love in his presence" (Eph. 1:4).

In the years that followed our Baptism, we grew in awareness—even wonder—of the mystery of Christ. By listening to the beatitudes, by meditating on the cross, conversing with Christ in prayer and receiving Him in the Eucharist, we progressed toward the day, that particular moment of our life, when we solemnly ratified with full awareness and freedom our baptismal consecration. We affirmed our determination to live always in union with Christ, and to be, according to the gifts given us by the Holy Spirit, a generous and loving member of the People of God.

2. Your religious consecration builds on this common foundation which all Christians share in the Body of Christ. Desiring to perfect and intensify what God had begun in your life by Baptism, and discerning that God was indeed offering you the gift of the evangelical counsels, you willed to follow Christ more closely, to conform your life more completely to that of Jesus Christ, in and through a distinctive religious community. This is the essence of religious consecration: to profess within and for the benefit of the Church, poverty, chastity and obedience in response to God's special invitation, in order to praise and serve God in greater freedom of heart (cf. 1 Cor. 7:34-35) and to have one's life more closely conformed to Christ in the manner of life chosen by Him and His Blessed Mother (cf. *Perfectae caritatis*, no. 1; *Lumen gentium*, no. 46).

3. Religious consecration not only deepens your personal commitment to Christ, but it also strengthens your relationship to His spouse, the Church. Religious consecration is a distinctive manner of living in the Church, a particular way of fulfilling the life of faith and service begun in Baptism.

On her part, the Church assists you in your discernment of God's will. Having accepted and authenticated the charisms of your various institutes, she then unites your religious profession to the celebration of Christ's paschal mystery.

You are called by Jesus Himself to verify and manifest in your lives and in your activities your deepened relationship with His Church. This bond of union with the Church must also be shown in the spirit and apostolic endeavors of every religious institute. For faithfulness to Christ, especially in religious life, can never be separated from faithfulness to the Church. This ecclesial dimension of the vocation of religious consecration has many important practical consequences for institutes themselves and for each individual member. It implies, for example, a greater public witness to the Gospel, since you represent, in a special way as women religious, the spousal relationship of the Church to Christ. The ecclesial dimension also requires, on the part of individual members as well as entire institutes, a faithfulness to the original charisms which God has given to His Church, through your founders and foundresses. It means that institutes are called to continue to foster, in dynamic faithfulness, those corporate commitments which were related to the original charism, which were authenticated by the Church, and which still fulfill important needs of the People of God. A good example in this regard would be the Catholic school system which has been invaluable for the Church in the United States, an excellent means not only for communicating the Gospel of Christ to the students, but also for permeating the entire community with Christ's truth and His love. It is one of the apostolates in which women religious have made, and are still making an incomparable contribution.

4. Dear sisters in Christ: Jesus must always be first in your lives. His Person must be at the center of your activities—the activities of every day. No other person and no other activity can take precedence over Him. For your whole life has been consecrated to Him. With St. Paul you have to say: "All I want is to know Christ and the power of his resurrection and to share his sufferings by reproducing the pattern of his death" (Phil. 3:10).

Christ remains primary in your life only when He enjoys the first place in your mind and heart. Thus you must continuously unite yourself to Him in prayer. Without prayer, religious life has no meaning. It has lost contact with its source, it has emptied itself of substance, and it no longer can fulfill its goal. Without prayer there can be no joy, no hope, no peace. For prayer is what keeps us in touch with Christ. The incisive words written in *Evangelica testificatio* cause us all to reflect: "Do not forget the witness of history: faithfulness to prayer or its abandonment is the test of the vitality or decadence of religious life" (*Evangelica testificatio,* no. 42).

5. Two dynamic forces are operative in religious life: your love for Jesus—and, in Jesus, for all who belong to Him—and His love for you.

We cannot live without love. If we do not encounter love, if we do not experience it and make it our own, and if we do not participate intimately in it, our life is meaningless. Without love we remain incomprehensible to ourselves (cf. *Redemptor hominis*, no. 10).

Thus every one of you needs a vibrant relationship of love with the Lord, a profound loving union with Christ, your Spouse, a love like that expressed in the psalm: "God, you are my God whom I seek, for you my flesh pines and my soul thirsts like the earth, parched, lifeless and without water. Thus have I gazed toward you in the sanctuary to see your power and your glory" (Ps. 63:1-2).

Yet far more important than your love for Christ is Christ's love for you. You have been called by Him, made a member of His Body, consecrated in a life of the evangelical counsels and destined by Him to have a share in the mission that Christ has entrusted to the Church: His own mission of salvation. For this reason, you center your life in the Eucharist. In the Eucharist, you celebrate His death and resurrection and receive from Him the Bread of eternal life. And it is in the Eucharist especially that you are united to the One who is the object of all your love. Here, with Him, you find ever greater reasons to love and serve His brothers and sisters. Here, with Him— with Christ—you find greater understanding and compassion for God's people. And here you find the strength to persevere in your commitment to selfless service.

6. Your service in the Church is then an extension of Christ, to whom you have dedicated your life. For it is not yourself that you put forward, but Christ Jesus as Lord. Like John the

Baptist, you know that for Christ to increase, you must decrease. And so your life must be characterized by a complete availability: a readiness to serve as the needs of the Church require, a readiness to give public witness to the Christ whom you love.

The need for this public witness becomes a constant call to inner conversion, to justice and holiness of life on the part of each religious. It also becomes an invitation to each institute to reflect on the purity of its corporate ecclesial witness. And it is for this reason that in my address last November to the international Union of Superiors General I mentioned that it is not unimportant that your consecration to God should be manifested in the permanent exterior sign of a simple and suitable religious garb. This is not only my personal conviction, but also the desire of the Church, often expressed by so many of the faithful.

As daughters of the Church—a title cherished by so many of your great saints—you are called to a generous and loving adherence to the authentic magisterium of the Church, which is a solid guarantee of the fruitfulness of all your apostolates and an indispensable condition for the proper interpretation of the "signs of the times."

7. The contemplative life occupies today and forever a place of great honor in the Church. The prayer of contemplation was found in the life of Jesus Himself, and has been a part of religious life in every age. I take this opportunity therefore—as I did in Rome, in Mexico and in Poland

—to encourage again all who are members of contemplative communities. Know that you shall always fulfill an important place in the Church, in her mission of salvation, in her service to the whole community of the People of God. Continue faithfully, confidently and prayerfully in the rich tradition that has been handed down to you.

In closing, I remind you, with sentiments of admiration and love, that the aim of religious life is to render praise and glory to the most holy Trinity, and, through your consecration, to help humanity enter into fullness of life in the Father, and in the Son and in the Holy Spirit. In all your planning and in all your activities, try also to keep this aim before you. There is no greater service you can give; there is no greater fulfillment you can receive. Dear sisters, today and forever: Praised be Jesus Christ!

Thank You, Mother, for This Presence of Yours

After his address to the religious, Pope John Paul spoke to all present on devotion to Mary and its significance for the many people who have come here from various countries of the world and built a new society. His address was a prayer to the Mother of God.

This Shrine speaks to us with the voice of all America, with the voice of all the sons and daughters of America, who have come here from the various countries of the Old World. When they came, they brought with them in their hearts the same love for the Mother of God that was a characteristic of their ancestors and of themselves in their native lands. These people, speaking different languages, coming from different backgrounds of history and tradition in their own countries, came together around the heart of a Mother whom they all had in common. While their faith in Christ made all of them aware of being the one People of God, this awareness became all the more vivid through the presence of the Mother in the work of Christ and the Church.

Today, as I thank you, Mother, for this presence of yours in the midst of the men and women of this land—a presence which has lasted two hundred years—giving a new form to their social and civic lives in the United States, I commend them all to your Immaculate Heart.

With gratitude and joy I recall that you have been honored as Patroness of the United States, under the title of your Immaculate Conception, since the days of the Sixth Provincial Council of Baltimore in 1846.

I commend to you, Mother of Christ, and I entrust to you the Catholic Church: the bishops, priests, deacons, individual religious and religious institutes, the seminarians, vocations, and the apostolate of the laity in its various aspects.

In a special way, I entrust to you the well-being of the Christian families of this country, the innocence of children, the future of the young, the vocation of single men and women. I ask you to communicate to all the women of the United States a deep sharing in the joy that you experienced in your closeness to Jesus Christ, your Son. I ask you to preserve all of them in freedom from sin and evil, like the freedom which was yours in a unique way from that moment of supreme liberation in your Immaculate Conception.

I entrust to you the great work of ecumenism here, in this land, in which those who confess Christ belong to different Churches and communions. I do this in order that the words of Christ's prayer may be fulfilled: "That they may be one." I entrust to you the consciences of men and women and the voice of public opinion, in order that they may not be opposed to the law of God but follow it as the fount of truth and good.

I add to this, Mother, the great cause of justice and peace in the modern world, in order that the force and energy of love may prevail over hatred and destructiveness, and in order that the children of light may not lack concern for the welfare of the whole human family.

Mother, I commend and entrust to you all that goes to make up earthly progress, asking that it should not be one-sided, but that it should create conditions for the full spiritual advancement of individuals, families, communities and nations. I commend to you the poor, the suffering, the sick and the handicapped, the aging and the dying. I ask you to reconcile those in sin, to heal those in pain, and to uplift those who have lost their hope and joy. Show to those who struggle in doubt the light of Christ your Son.

Bishops of the Church in the United States have chosen your Immaculate Conception as the mystery to hold the patronage over the People of God in this land. May the hope contained in this mystery overcome sin and be shared by all the sons and daughters of America, and also by the whole human family. At a time when the struggle between good and evil, between the prince of darkness and father of lies and evangelical love is growing more acute, may the light of your Immaculate Conception show to all the way to grace and to salvation. Amen.

Sanctification—
the First Apostolic Duty

On October 10, 1979, the Holy Father gave the follow-ing address to religious major superiors at the general audience.

There are present at the audience about six hundred women superiors general and provin-cials, who are taking part in the twenty-seventh assembly of the "Union of Major Superiors of Ita-ly" (USMI),-which has dealt with the subject: "The pastoral presence of religious in the Church of Italy today and their specific charism."

I thank you for your presence, such a sig-nificant one, which would have merited a private audience. Unfortunately, the multiple and ur-gent tasks of this period of time did not make it possible for me.

I exhort you, beloved sisters, to meditate always, with love and generosity, on the great documents which concern your life: the sixth chapter of the conciliar Constitution *Lumen gentium*, the Decree *Perfectae caritatis*, and the Apostolic Letter *Evangelica testificatio*. What I was most anxious to communicate to you and to all sisters, I expressed recently in the addresses delivered on October 1 at Maynooth in Ireland and on October 7 in the Shrine of the Immaculate Conception, in Washington.

Now, I would like just to suggest to you su-periors the firmness and delicacy necessary at this moment. Show yourselves above all to be mothers, sensitive and enlightened, never irritated or embittered by anything, but holily intrepid in following the voice of the Vicar of Christ, so that no sister will feel depressed or excluded, even if she may have made some mistake.

I repeat to you, too, what I said in Ireland: "You must be courageous in your apostolic undertakings, not letting difficulties, shortage of personnel, insecurity for the future, deter or depress you. Always remember that the first apostolic duty is your sanctification" (Address at Maynooth, October 1, 1979).

May my apostolic blessing be particularly close to you and comforting.

On Catechesis in Our Time

The following is an excerpt from the Apostolic Exhortation of Pope John Paul II, Catechesi tradendae, *issued on October 16, 1979.*

Many religious institutes for men and women came into being for the purpose of giving Christian education to children and young people, especially the most abandoned. Throughout history, men and women religious have been deeply committed to the Church's catechetical activity, doing particularly apposite and effective work. At a time when it is desired that the links between religious and pastors should be accentuated and consequently the active presence of religious communities and their members in the pastoral projects of the local Churches, I wholeheartedly exhort you, whose religious consecration should make you even more readily available for the Church's service, to prepare as well as possible for the task of catechesis according to the differing vocations in your institutes and the missions entrusted to you, and to carry this concern everywhere. Let the communities dedicate as much as possible of what ability and means they have to the specific work of catechesis.

Be Friends of Jesus

On October 21, 1979, after entering the Basilica of Our Lady of the Rosary of Pompei, the Holy Father knelt in prayer before the picture of the Madonna. In the Basilica he met the bishops of Campania, led by Cardinal Corrado Ursi, Archbishop of Naples; Cardinal Mozzoni, President of the Cardinalitial Commission for the Pontifical Sanctuaries of Pompei and Loreto, priests and men and women religious. His Holiness spoke to those present. The following is an excerpt.

My greeting goes also to you, beloved sisters, who perpetuate the extraordinary spiritual heritage of your Founder, the Venerable Bartolo Longo, his message and his examples of faith and charity. He, as is known, driven by his ardent devotion to the Mother of God, and trusting in divine Providence, in May, 1876, began the construction of this temple, famous all over the world today. But around the Shrine he wished to create a whole series of admirable educational and charitable works, particularly in favor of children, so much so that this complex was defined "the living citadel of charity." At the basis of all these works, there was the Venerable's deep conviction that he who loves God also loves his neighbor (cf. 1 Jn. 4:21).

Therefore, in your religious consecration, practice love of God, to whom you have given your whole life, your whole heart, your whole will; but practice also, no less intensely and concretely, love of needy brothers, especially children, with generous availability and immense joy, aware that "he who loves his neighbor has fulfilled the law" (Rom. 13:8).

We Must Be for Others

During his pastoral visit to St. Pius V parish on October 28, 1979, Pope John Paul II met the priests and representatives of the religious communities of men and of women residing in the area, and delivered the following address.

Beloved brothers and sisters in the Lord,

In this pastoral visit of mine, it was essential to have a special meeting with all of you, priests and religious men and women, who are numerous in this parish.

Therefore I happily find myself here with you, and express my joy to you all as a father, a brother and a friend: and at this short meeting I would like to suggest to you some thoughts that rise from the demands of our time.

What is the general characteristic of the time in which Providence has called upon us to live? It seems that we can answer that it is a great spiritual crisis: of intelligence, of religious faith and, consequently, of moral life.

We are called to live in this age of ours and therefore to love it in order to save it. What, then, does it require us to do?

1. *Our time calls in the first place for deep philosophical and theological convictions.*

Many failures in faith and in consecrated life, past and recent, and many present situations of distress and perplexity, have their origin in a crisis of a philosophical nature. It is necessary to dedicate serious efforts to one's own cultural formation. The Second Vatican Council stressed the necessity of always keeping St. Thomas Aquinas as both teacher and doctor, because it is only in the light and on the basis of "perennial philosophy" that the edifice of Christian doctrine, both logical and demanding, can be founded. Leo XIII, of venerated memory, in his famous Encyclical *Aeterni Patris*, which still is relevant today, the centenary of which falls this year, stressed and illustrated in an admirable way the validity of the rational foundation for Christian faith.

Today, therefore, our first concern must be with truth, both for our interior needs and for our ministry. We cannot sow error or leave people in the shadow of doubt! Christian faith of the hereditary and sociological type becomes more and more personal, interior, demanding, and this is certainly a good thing, but we must *have* in order to be able to give! Let us remember what St. Paul wrote to his disciple, Timothy: "Guard what has been entrusted to you. Avoid the godless chatter and contradictions of what is falsely called knowledge, for by professing it some have missed the mark as regards the faith" (1 Tm. 6:20).

It is a valid exhortation, especially for our time, which is so thirsty for certainty and charity and so deeply threatened and tormented.

2. *Our time calls for mature and well-balanced personalities.*

Ideological confusion gives rise to personalities that are immature and inadequate psychologically; pedagogy itself is seen to be uncertain and sometimes deviated. For this very reason the modern world is in painful pursuit of ideals, and

WE MUST BE FOR OTHERS   225

as often as not is left disappointed, defeated and humiliated. Therefore we must be mature personalities, who are able to control our sensitivity, assume our own roles of responsibility and guidance, and try to reach fulfillment in the place and work in which we find ourselves.

Our time calls for serenity and courage to accept reality as it is, without depressing criticisms and without utopias, in order to love it and save it.

Endeavor, therefore, all of you, to reach these ideals of "maturity," through love of duty, meditation, spiritual reading, examination of conscience, the methodical use of the sacrament of Penance, and spiritual direction. The Church and modern society need mature personalities: we must be so, with God's help!

3. *Finally, our time calls for a serious commitment with regard to our own sanctification.*

The spiritual necessities of the present-day world are immense! If we look at the boundless forests of buildings in modern metropolises, invaded by numberless multitudes, we cannot but be frightened. How can we reach these persons and bring them to Christ?

We are helped by the certainty of being only instruments of grace: it is God Himself who acts in the individual soul, with His love and His mercy.

Our real and constant goal must be that of personal sanctification, to be suitable and effective instruments of grace.

The truest and most sincere wish I can form for you is just this: "Make yourselves saints and do so quickly!", while I repeat to you the words of St. Paul to the Thessalonians: "May the God of peace himself sanctify you wholly; and may your spirit and soul and body be kept sound and blameless at the coming of our Lord Jesus Christ" (1 Thes. 5:23).

Beloved in Christ!

Let us be happy to live in these times of ours and let us commit ourselves courageously to the plan that Providence carries out mysteriously, also through us.

St. Pius V, "whose outstanding figure"—John XXIII said—"is united with the great ordeals that the Church had to go through in times far more difficult than our own" (Discorsi, messaggi e colloqui, vol. II, p. 720, May 6, 1960), teaches us, too, to have recourse in our difficulties to holy Mary, our heavenly Mother, who overcomes all errors and all heresies. Let us pray to her always, let us pray to her especially with the holy rosary, in order that our one supreme ideal may always be the salvation of souls.

I willingly impart to you my special apostolic blessing.

United in Truth and Charity for a Consistent Implementation of Vatican Council II

With the Holy Father, there were present 120 Cardinals at the opening of the plenary meeting of the Sacred College in the Synod Hall on November 5, 1979. After an address of homage by the Cardinal Dean, Pope John Paul II delivered a discourse, of which the following is an excerpt.

The most important conclusion concerns *the proper understanding and exercise of freedom in the Church.* The Council, following the words of the Lord, desires to serve the development of this freedom—the freedom of the children of God, which in our own times, especially, has great significance, inasmuch as we are witnesses of many ways in which people are subjected to constraint, including constraint of their consciences and hearts. One must never forget that the Lord said: "You will know the truth, and the truth will make you free" (Jn. 8:32). For this reason the Church must preserve in the heart and conscience of each of her sons and daughters, and also, if possible, in the heart and conscience of every human being, the truth about freedom itself. Very often, freedom of will and the freedom of the person are understood as *the right to do anything,* as the right not to accept any norm or any duty that involves commitment also in the dimension of the whole of life, for example the duties following from the marriage promises or from priestly ordination. *But Christ does not teach us such an interpretation and exercise of freedom.* The freedom of each individual creates duties, demands full respect for the hierarchy of values, and is potentially directed to the good without limits, to God. In Christ's eyes, freedom is not first of all "freedom from" but "freedom for." The full enjoyment of freedom is love, in particular the love through which individuals give themselves. Man, in fact, as we read in the same chapter of *Gaudium et spes,* "cannot fully find himself except through a sincere gift of himself" (no. 24).

It is this interpretation and this exercise of freedom that must be present at the basis of the whole work of renewal. Only the individual who understands and exercises his or her freedom in the manner indicated by Christ opens his or her spirit to the working of the Holy Spirit, who is the Spirit of truth and love. On the authentic affirmation of the freedom of the children of God depends the great work of *vocations,* to the priesthood, the religious life, marriage. On it also depends effective ecumenical progress, and the whole of Christian witness, that is to say, the sharing of Christians in the cause of making the world more human. This is the first condition.

Religious Witness
in Keeping with Our Time

The work of the Fifth General Assembly of the International Union of Women Superiors General (UISG) ended with a concelebrated Mass presided over by the Holy Father in the Sistine Chapel on November 14, 1979.

Pope John Paul II delivered the following homily.

Dear sisters in the Lord,

It is a great joy for me to meet you today, you who are particularly authorized representatives of the great riches that religious life constitutes in the Church. By means of it, in fact, a particularly evident testimony is offered of what complete donation to love and service of God means. I am happy at the same time to see and greet in you, as it were, the image of the universality of the Church. You represent here all the continents and the various cultures, and you manifest together the multiform realization of the response to the Lord's call.

Through you I wish to affirm again to all sisters the appreciation and trust that the Church has in them, not only on account of their intelligent, constant and generous apostolate, but even more because of their life of consecration, of dedication that is very often concealed, and of joyful and courageous acceptance of the inevitable trials and difficulties. I ask you to transmit my very special blessing to all sisters sorely tried or exhausted in body and in spirit, to the old and the sick, whose lives of abnegation and sacrifice are an extremely precious, unique value—not to be renounced—for the Church, the Pope and the People of God.

I wish further that this Eucharistic Celebration together with the Pope will be for each of you a salutary moment of encouragement and comfort in the accomplishment of a commitment that is always demanding, often accompanied by the sign of the cross and by painful solitude, and which calls on your side for a deep sense of responsibility, a generosity without weakness or confusion, and constant forgetfulness of yourselves. You, in fact, must sustain and guide your fellow sisters in this post-conciliar period, which is certainly rich in new experiences, but also so exposed to errors and deviations, which you try to avoid and correct. We all know the positive evolution of the last few years in religious life, which is interpreted with a more evangelical, more ecclesial and more apostolic spirit. However, it cannot be ignored that certain practical choices, even if prompted by good, but not always enlightened intentions, have not offered the world the true image of Christ, whom the religious sisters should make present among men.

Finding yourselves gathered round the altar to renew Christ's offering to the Father, you feel yourselves intimately invited to repeat, also on behalf of your fellow sisters, the consecration of yourselves which, already begun with Baptism, was made definitive and perfect by means of the religious vows.

1. Take to heart, therefore, my first exhortation to fervent and persevering prayer, in order that the importance of the religious vocation and the necessity of examining thoroughly its essential value, in the life of the Church and of society, may be more and more evident. The life story of every woman religious, in fact, is centered on the nuptial love for Christ, as a result of which she, modeled by His Spirit, gives Him her whole life, adopting His sentiments, His ideals and His mission of charity and salvation. As I said already to the sisters in Ireland: "No movement in religious life has any importance unless it be also movement inwards to the 'still center' of your existence, where Christ is. It is not what you *do* that matters most; but what you *are,* as women consecrated to God" (Address to priests and men and women religious of Ireland, October 1, 1979).

—Pray that every sister, living joyfully her unique and faithful relationship with Christ, may find in her consecration the highest fulfillment of her own characteristic reality as a woman, which seeks expression in self-giving.

—Pray confidently that every institute may easily overcome its difficulties of growth and perseverance and that your annual meeting may contribute to an ever greater perfecting of the individual congregations to which you belong.

—Finally, pray uninterruptedly for religious vocations: may the ideal of consecrated life, an immense and gratuitous gift from God, exert an ever greater attraction on numerous young women, straining towards the highest and most noble achievements.

May the subject chosen by the Sacred Congregation for Religious and for Secular Institutes for the next plenary meeting: "The contemplative dimension of religious life," be a very special opportunity to become more deeply aware of the fundamental value of prayer. In this connection, I intend to address a fervent thought and a blessing to sisters of contemplative life, whom I thank warmly for their intense and constant prayer, which is an irreplaceable help in the Church's mission of evangelization.

2. My second exhortation, now, is a call to commit yourselves to religious witness in keeping with our time.

After the years of experience, aimed at updating religious life, according to the spirit of the institute, the time has come to evaluate objectively and humbly the attempts made, to recognize their positive elements, and any deviations, and finally to prepare a *rule of stable life,* approved by the Church, which should constitute for all the sisters a stimulus to deeper knowledge of their commitments and to joyful faithfulness in living them.

Let the first witness be that of filial adherence and unfailing faithfulness to the Church, Christ's bride. This link with the Church must be manifested in the spirit of your institute and in its tasks of apostolate, because faithfulness to Christ can never be separated from faithfulness to the Church. "You are called to a generous and loving adherence to the authentic magisterium of the Church, which is a solid guarantee of the fruitfulness of all your apostolates and an indispensable condition for the proper interpretation of the 'signs of the times' " (Address to women religious of the United States, October 7, 1979).

In imitation of Mary, the Virgin whose heart was always open to God's word, you must find your inner serenity, your joy, in availability for the word of the Church and of him whom Christ has placed as His Vicar on earth.

Let a second witness be that of community life.

The latter, in fact, is an important element of religious life. It has been a characteristic of the lives of religious persons from the beginning, because spiritual bonds cannot be created, developed and perpetuated unless through daily and prolonged relations. This community life, in evangelical charity, is closely linked with the mystery of the Church, which is a mystery of communion and participation, and gives proof of your consecration to Christ. Make every effort that this community life may be facilitated and loved, becoming in this way a precious means of mutual help and personal fulfillment.

Finally, as I have already said on other occasions, a last, special witness is also that of a religious garb. It constitutes, in fact, an evident sign of complete consecration to the ideals of the kingdom of heaven, always considering all due circumstances, such as, for example, tradition, the various fields of apostolic commitment, the environment, etc. It is also a sign of definitive detachment from merely human and earthly interests; it is a sign, furthermore, of poverty lived joyfully and loved in confident abandonment to God's provident action.

Beloved Superiors General, you must assume the delicate and sometimes difficult, but also precious, task of promoting among religious women everything that can contribute to the union of minds and hearts. A sisterly, fervent and authentic life is indispensable in order that women religious may cope in a lasting way with the obligations, toil and difficulties that a life of consecration and apostolate entails in the world of today.

Your task in the happy realization of such a life, deeply rooted in evangelical values, is of the utmost importance. The exercise of authority, in a spirit of service and love for all fellow sisters, is a vital task, even though a difficult one, which calls for no little courage and dedication. The superior has the duty to help the sister to realize her vocation more and more perfectly. She cannot shirk this obligation, which is certainly an arduous one, but indispensable.

To carry out this duty calls for constant prayer, reflection, consultation, but also *courageous decisions,* in awareness of your responsibility before God, the Church and the sisters themselves who expect this service. Weakness, like authoritarianism, are deviations that are equally harmful for the good of souls and the proclamation of the kingdom.

3. In conclusion, I exhort you affectionately: have confidence. Always be courageous in your religious dedication; do not become disheartened

by possible difficulties, by the reduction of personnel and by uncertainties as regards the future. Do not doubt *the validity of tested forms of apostolate* in the field of education of the young, for the sick, children, the old and all those who are suffering.

Be certain that if your institutes strive sincerely to promote among the sisters constant, generous and dynamic faithfulness to the requirements of their consecrated life, the Lord, who does not let Himself be outdone in generosity, will send you the desired vocations you await for the advent of His kingdom.

Attentive to the suggestions and to the words of Wisdom, as is fitting for persons called to carry out a high responsibility of government, and grateful to God—together with all your fellow sisters—for the special vocation you have received, walk with serene confidence along the path of your commitment of total consecration to Christ and to souls. May the most holy Mary, the Mother and model of all consecrated persons, strengthen you and sustain you, and may my apostolic blessing accompany you with special benevolence.

Intense Work for Native Vocations

On November 20, 1979, the Holy Father received in audience a group of bishops and of prelates of various vicariates and prefectures apostolic of Colombia, on their visit ad limina Apostolorum. *The following is an excerpt of the address which Pope John Paul II delivered.*

A special note characterizes our meeting today, since you, beloved brothers, as prelates of the various vicariates apostolic and prefectures apostolic of Colombia, bring to me the specific presence of the missionary Church in your country.

Consequently, my first word is one of esteem and thanks for your commitment in the work of building and consolidating the Church in each of the ecclesial districts entrusted to your pastoral care and responsibility.

In this task, such a vital and meritorious one, you receive precious help from the congregations and religious institutes to which your missionary districts are entrusted. I wish, consequently, to express here my sincere appreciation and gratitude, to which I add the testimony of my deep satisfaction and praise, to the members of these well-deserving religious families, who spend such generous energies in this task in the midst of so many environmental difficulties and not a few privations. May the Lord reward them abundantly! These are sentiments which

extend to all the others—sisters particularly—
who work with abnegation in close collaboration
with you.

THE WHOLE DIOCESE
SHOULD BE MISSIONARY

I know that you are engaged in the work of
intense cultivation of native vocations. That
makes me really very happy and I encourage you
to spare no effort in continuing along this way,
which goes in the direction of the essential and
prior needs of the Church.

However, looking at the overall panorama of
the Church in your nation, we could ask ourselves if other more privileged dioceses were not
able to offer you valuable help, by generously
putting at your disposal personnel of evangelization, particularly priests and religious, which it
seems they are in a position to give you.

This brotherly help between the various ecclesial communities, as well as being an evident
sign of communion in Christ and maturity in the
experience of the Catholic Faith, as well as con-
tributing to correct quite considerable inequali-
ties as regards evangelizing forces, would greatly
aid the elevation of your missionary districts to
dioceses of common law, an aim to which I myself look with favor and which I greatly desire, as
soon as circumstances permit.

Active consciousness of the help that a particular church can and must give to another one,
less privileged as regards pastoral agents and
even material resources, far from reducing its

own energies, will give it a new lease on life, by bringing forth new forces of ecclesial generosity and fruitfulness, as a reward for its own openness in the dynamic charity of the Gospel and a seed of certain divine blessings.

Then, too, if the missionary dimension is a necessary consequence of Christian vocation, and if "the whole Church is missionary, and the work of evangelization the fundamental task of the People of God" (*Ad gentes*, no. 35), every diocesan community—with its respective pastor, priests, men and women religious, seminarians and laity—must implement these vast ecclesial aims, which extend to other brother communities in the Faith.

There is a fine evangelizing task here for everyone and more specifically for pastors, since, as the Second Vatican Council recalls, "by arousing, fostering and directing missionary work in his own diocese,...the bishop makes present and, as it were, visible the missionary spirit and zeal of the People of God, so that the whole diocese becomes missionary" (*Ad gentes*, no. 38).

Let not Projection
Towards the Future
Destroy the Acquired Heritage

On November 26, 1979, the Holy Father received members of the Council of the Union of Men Superiors General, who were accompanied by Cardinal Eduardo Pironio, Prefect of the Sacred Congregation for Religious and for Secular Institutes.

John Paul II delivered the following address.

Beloved brothers and sons!

1. Allow me to tell you openly my joy at receiving you today, in this house, as qualified members of the Council of the Union of Superiors General and therefore representatives of vast hosts of religious scattered all over the world. I thank you for having desired this meeting, which enables me to address my cordial word to you.

The organism of which you are the expression and which you represent, fosters not only greater fellowship among the various religious families, but also more compact action on their part within, and for the building up of, the holy Church. I hope it will always be so in actual fact.

My intention, here and now, is just to recall together with you some great aspects of religious life, which, by their nature, also inspire actual behavior. The conciliar Decree *Perfectae caritatis*, on the renewal of religious life, contains the following already in the introduction: "All those who are called by God to the practice of the evangelical counsels, and who make faithful profession of them,...live more and more for Christ and for His Body, the Church (cf. Col. 1:24). The more fervently, therefore, they join themselves to Christ by this gift of their whole life, the fuller does the Church's life become and the more vigorous and fruitful its apostolate" (no. 1).

SIGN OF PARTICIPATION

2. Beloved in Christ, you represent in the Church a state of life that goes back to the first centuries of her history and which has always expressed in turn, within the various religious families, abundant and savory fruit of holiness, incisive Christian witness, efficacious apostolate, and even a considerable contribution to the formation of a rich heritage of culture and civilization. Well, all this has been, and still is, possible precisely on the basis of that total and faithful union with Christ, of which the Council speaks, and which is not only asked of you but can also be favorably realized owing to the special status of religious consecrated to the Lord.

The charism peculiar to each of the institutes represented by you is an eloquent sign of participation in the multiform riches of Christ, the "breadth and length and height and depth" (Eph. 3:18) of which always far surpasses what we can realize when drawing upon their fullness. The Church, which is the visible face of Christ in time, receives, and nourishes within her, orders and institutes of such different style, because all together they contribute to revealing the variegated nature and the multiple dynamism of the Incarnate Word of God and of the community of believers in Him.

WITNESS AND COMMITMENT

3. But there is another reason above all which justifies and demands the religious state. In an age and a world in which there is a proximate danger of constructing man with one dimension only—which inevitably ends up by being the historicist and immanentist one—religious are called to keep high the value and the sense of worshiping prayer, not separated from, but united with, the living commitment of generous service to men, which draws possibilities and impetus precisely from this prayer.

It is a question of a program of life which it is particularly appropriate for religious, even more than for the secular clergy, to carry out and incarnate, by means of faithful and joyful observance of the evangelical counsels and with special emphasis on the immediate communion with Him "who dwells in unapproachable light, whom no man has ever seen or can see" (1 Tm. 6:16). Men must learn from you to pay Him "honor and eternal dominion" *(ibid.)*, without thereby creating sterile conflicts with their temporal commitments, so that, in fact, they may thus find a salutary way of bringing things into perspective and a fruitful direction of elevation towards Christ, in whom all things are united, "things in heaven and things on earth" (Eph. 1:10).

Today's society wishes to see in your families how much harmony exists between the human and the divine, between "things that are seen" and "things that are unseen" (1 Cor. 4:18), and how much the latter surpass the former, never making them trivial or humiliating them, but giving them new life and raising them in accordance with the eternal plan of salvation. Prayer and work, action and contemplation: they are dual concepts which, in Christ, never deteriorate into antithetical opposition, but mature, complementing and integrating each other fruitfully. Well, the task of the witness of religious is precisely this: to show the world of today how much humanity there is in the mystery of Christ (cf. Tit. 3:4) and at the same time how much commitment among men calls for the transcendental and the supernatural (cf. Ps. 127:1).

YARDSTICK OF BEHAVIOR

4. This harmonious synthesis is, after all, also the real reason for your impact and the attraction you exert on the men and especially the young of today. And it is also on the basis of a healthy balance between human and Christian values that religious life can be renewed and purified and shine forth more and more, as everyone desires. Of course, there will be no lack of difficulties, risks and tensions, which you well know. But we must not labor under the illusion of solving the inevitable problems from a purely

worldly standpoint or, on the contrary, a disembodied one. The most adequate yardstick of
behavior cannot but be the example of Jesus and
our pure faith in Him. It is from the Gospel, in
fact, that there comes our sense of unshakable
adherence to the Father's will and at the same
time a boldness, which, however, is not rash, in
our decisions, the sense of a courageous projec-
tion towards the future as well as prudent pres-
ervation of the rich spiritual heritage acquired in
the past.

No step forward is possible, in any direction,
unless starting from those already taken; but,
vice versa, to stop at the latter is a sign of sterile
stagnation. Furthermore, progress in an evangelical direction is certainly made at the level of
individual holiness, but also at that of public
witness to Christ. Now, He is the Lord of the
whole of human history, not only the past but
also the present and what still stretches out in
front of us, and therefore requires an adherence
that is always total but always adapted. The
Apostle Paul, reminding the Galatians that "in
Christ Jesus neither circumcision nor uncircum-
cision is of any avail, but faith working through
love" (Gal. 5:6), has given all Christians a fundamental hermeneutical principle for their existence in the world, a principle which must hold
good all the more clearly for religious. When one
"holds fast to the head," which is Christ (Col.
2:19), then one does not fear any changing historical conditioning, inculturation or obstacle,
since everything, on the contrary, becomes valid
material for inner progress, open witness and

apostolic efficacy; provided that everything "may increase thanksgiving, to the glory of God" (2 Cor. 4:15).

It is from here that we must all draw courage and confidence. From you, in particular, the Church expects a great deal by way of an impelling example of radical communion with Christ, which will naturally produce a generous commitment among men.

ASCETIC EFFORT NEEDED

5. I propose these thoughts to you and to all those you worthily represent, urging you to meditate on them and keep them always in mind, not only in specific moments of prayer, but also and particularly in carrying out, even in small matters, the various educative, welfare, cultural, missionary and promotional activities in general, which are such a distinctive mark of yours. Precisely in consecrated persons, more than in any other baptized persons, there must shine forth, as in Jesus, perfect symbiosis between moments of transfiguration (cf. Lk. 9:28-36) and those of deep integration among the demanding multitude, which waits at the foot of the mountain (cf. *ibid.*, 9:37-43).

If this task is not an easy one, if it requires a great ascetic effort and, even more, the abundant and indispensable grace of God, be certain that you do not lack my fatherly closeness and the comfort of my poor but constant prayer, in order that "the Lord make his face to shine upon you" (Nm. 6:25) and that in you, men may see "the light of the gospel showing forth the glory of Christ" (cf. 2 Cor. 4:4).

To these good wishes I am happy to add my special, apostolic blessing, in propitiation, and I extend it with equal benevolence to all your dear and well-deserving confreres.

Need of Greater Collaboration for a More Organic Apostolate

On January 4, 1980, the Holy Father received in audience participants in the first study and orientation meeting on the subject "Presence and mission of men and women religious in the diocese of Rome." Pope John Paul II delivered the following address.

Beloved sisters and brothers!

"Grace to you and peace from God our Father and the Lord Jesus Christ" (2 Cor. 1:2).

1. In this Christmas period and beginning of the new year, it is a deep joy for me to be able to meet you, men and women religious, living and operating in Rome, the diocese of the Pope.

At this moment I would like to greet all of you, not only according to religious families, but also individually, to tell you, with simplicity and sincerity, my appreciation for you all and for the fundamental choice you have made of your life, giving it completely and unconditionally to God, to Christ and to the Church; and furthermore to express to you my encouragement in order that you may continue to offer, with the same commitment and enthusiasm as in the first days, your testimony of religious and evangelical life in modern society, which is more and more thirsty for God and seeking to give its own choices a deep and real meaning.

My brotherly greeting goes to you men and women religious, who, uniting contemplation and action in a fruitful synthesis, dedicate all your energies to proclamation of the evangelical message in catechesis and in school teaching, or in the various forms of love for man in the multiple charitable initiatives which have sprung from the hearts of your founders and foundresses, in particular in the various types of assistance for children, the old, the sick and the deprived, etc. Illuminated by faith, you see in them the image of Christ; that same Christ whom you, by response to an inner call, have followed generously along the way of the cross, self-giving and suffering. You have understood and put into practice the words of St. Augustine: *Ille unus quaerendus est, qui et redemit et liberos fecit, et sanguinem suum ut eos emeret dedit, et servos suos fratres fecit* (It is necessary to seek only Him who redeemed and liberated and shed his blood to ransom them and made those who were slaves his brothers: *Enarr. in Ps.* 34, 15, *Serm.* I: *PL* 36, 333).

By seeking and following Christ, particularly in chastity, poverty and obedience, you give the world a concrete testimony of the primacy of spiritual life, as the Second Vatican Council effectively stressed: "They who make profession of the evangelical counsels should seek and love above all else God who first loved us (cf. 1 John 4:10). In all circumstances they should take care to foster a life hidden with Christ in God (cf. Col. 3:3), which is the source and stimulus of love of neighbor, for the salvation of the world and the building up of the Church" (Decree *Perfectae caritatis*, no. 6). And bear witness also to hope in the risen Christ.

REFLECTING TOGETHER

2. In these days you are gathered for a study and orientation meeting, the subject of which is the presence and mission of men and women religious in the diocese of Rome, in order to meditate and reflect together on the document *Mutuae relationes*. This meeting, the first of its kind, was suggested, proposed and desired by you. I cannot but express my cordial congratulations on this praiseworthy and exemplary pastoral and ecclesial sensitivity of yours.

There is no doubt that men and women religious constitute great riches and considerable power for the universal Church and for the particular Churches, owing in the first place to the immense spiritual good they have done and continue to do, taking inspiration from the specific purposes of their institutes, but also owing to the various works and instruments at their disposal for the good of souls. This power and these riches can and must be used in a more and more effective way for the apostolate and they can and must become living and vital elements in the diocesan apostolate as a whole, at all levels.

WORKING IN THE DIOCESE

3. As is known, the Second Vatican Council, dealing with religious life, tackled on several occasions the problem of the integration and collaboration of men religious—and therefore also women religious in the same way—in the life of

the individual dioceses. The Council speaks exactly of the "necessary...unity and harmony in the carrying out of apostolic work" (Dogmatic Constitution *Lumen gentium*, no. 45); it defines religious priests as "prudent cooperators with the episcopal order" (Decree *Christus Dominus*, no. 34), and states that "the other members too of the religious institutes, both men and women, also belong in a special sense to the diocesan family and render valuable help to the sacred hierarchy, and in view of the growing needs of the apostolate they can and should constantly increase the aid they give" *(ibid.)*. This pastoral cooperation must, of course, take place in respect of the character and the constitutions of each religious institute.

This collaboration within the particular Church will certainly lead to a coordination of initiatives, which will avoid cases of overlapping, useless and costly in personnel and energies; but in particular it will give the unified direction of a consistent finality to be reached *collatis consiliis* and *viribus unitis.* All that, we cannot conceal, may also involve and require sacrifices: full availability for the implementation of a more organic and functional pastoral plan, that is, of that *ratio pastoralis* of which the Apostolic Constitution *Vicariae potestatis* speaks (no. 2:7); the capacity to renounce particular initiatives and projects, which would not be adequately integrated, perhaps, in an "overall pastoral plan." But these are sacrifices which are certainly fruitful for the real good of souls and for the edification of the Church.

DIOCESAN PROBLEMS

4. In these days of common prayer and intense study, various specialists will study the conciliar texts I have referred to, as well as the above-mentioned document *Mutuae relationes,* in order that, in the vast and complex diocese of Rome, the numerically important presence of religious men and women may constitute a proof and a sign of apostolic ardor and a valuable aid to tackle and solve, realistically, the various problems which emerge from the socio-cultural context of the city and which are analyzed by your study groups: the problems of ongoing catechesis; culture; the world of work; schools; politics; assistance for the suburbs; educational and welfare institutes; prayer centers; priestly and religious vocations; addiction to drugs; the missions; and so many others, which will certainly crop up in your serene and frank discussions.

I am relying a great deal on your proven generosity and your love for the Church, in order that, by means of your eager and efficient collaboration, there can be applied also to the Romans of today the words that St. Paul addressed to the first Christians of the capital of the Empire: "I thank my God through Jesus Christ for all of you, because your faith is proclaimed in all the world" (Rom. 1:8).

Take heart! It is a question, once more, of following Christ, walking with Him, in spite of the inevitable sacrifices. But let us listen to and treasure St. Augustine's recommendation: *Am-*

bula securus in Christo, ambula; ne offendas, ne cadas, ne retro respicias, ne in via emaneas, ne a via recedas (Walk confidently in Christ, walk; do not stumble, do not fall, do not look back, do not stop on the way, do not take another path: *Serm.* 170, 11: *PL* 38, 932).

With my apostolic blessing.

God Loves a Cheerful Giver

On January 12, 1980, the Holy Father received about a thousand religious brothers of clerical and lay institutes of Rome. There were present at the audience, the first of the kind ever granted by a Pope, numerous Superiors General of the various religious congregations, led by Cardinal Eduardo Pironio, Prefect of the Sacred Congregation for Religious and for Secular Institutes.

John Paul II delivered the following address.

Beloved sons!

1. I am really happy to meet you this morning in the familiarity of this audience. I attach a special significance and affection to this talk. Today it is actually entirely for you, lay brothers of the various congregations, whose contribution is so important for the life and activity of the respective religious families, and, more in general, for the life of the whole Church. Receiving you, it is my intention to stress the appreciation that the Church has for your function, and to give space to some reflections which will highlight the specific aspects of your choice of life.

Opening to you, therefore, the doors of my house, beloved brothers, I also open my heart and address to you an affectionate greeting which, through your persons, is intended to reach all lay religious brothers scattered over the world, and to bring them the testimony of my sincere esteem and high appreciation.

JOY IN BEING A CONSECRATED PERSON

2. You are called to walk towards perfection along the way of the evangelical counsels, professed with generous totality of commitment. You are, in fact, fully "religious." The Second Vatican Council, as you know, solemnly confirmed the principle according to which your choice of life "is a state for the profession of the evangelical counsels which is complete in itself" (Decree *Perfectae caritatis,* no. 10) and it has a special word to "confirm" you in your vocation (cf. *ibid.),* in order that, from renewed "certainty" about the validity of your commitment, there might be derived a strengthening of resolutions and a more generous impetus of creative dynamism.

Renew in yourselves, therefore, the awareness and joy of your state as consecrated persons; Christ must be the purpose and the measure of your lives. Your vocation had its origin in the meeting with Him: faith in Him determined the "yes" of your commitment, the hope of His help now supports its persevering fulfillment, the love that He has lit in your hearts nourishes the enthusiasm necessary for overcoming inevitable difficulties and for the daily renewal of your offer.

A CALL TO GREATER SERVICE

3. In Christ, who "came down from heaven for us men and for our salvation," you have also discovered the deep reason for your gift to your brothers. This is a point that deserves a stop for

reflection. Your religious consecration not only strengthened the baptismal gift of union with the Trinity, but also called you to greater service of the People of God.

You must live your service, whatever it may be, with your spirit open to the whole Church: you contribute to her life with your activity and with your witness (cf. *Lumen gentium*, no. 44). Here it is opportune to come down to concrete matters, in the attempt to shed light on some characteristic aspects of the riches which your life as lay religious brothers represents for the Church.

Your religious profession is set, in the first place, in the line of baptismal consecration, and expresses the bipolarity of the universal priesthood, which is based on this consecration. In life as lay religious, in fact, there takes place the offering of the spiritual sacrifice, the exercise of worship in spirit and truth, to which every Christian is called; at the same time, there rings out in it before the world a very clear proclamation of the marvels of salvation. A double direction, therefore, towards God and towards men, characterizes your life; and at the basis of both there is the same one baptismal priesthood, in both there is expressed the same love spread in the heart by the Spirit (cf. Rom. 5:5), in both there is lived in fullness the identical charism of the "laity," conferred by the grace of the sacraments of Christian initiation.

There is more. The text of the Decree *Perfectae caritatis* points out a particular form of "ecclesial service" which lay religious are called to carry out. They take part in a very useful way "in the exercise of its (the Church's) pastoral duty of educating the young, caring for the sick, and in its other ministries" (no. 10), which are not further specified, but which each of you can well exemplify, thinking of the activity you carry out. Well, it is important that each of you should be fully aware of the essentially ecclesial character of your work, whatever it may be.

This is true above all since according to the interior dynamics of grace, your religious consecration, by its nature, directs to the life of the Mystical Body every form of activity to which you are called in virtue of obedience. The believer is well aware that the importance of his own contribution to the life of the Church does not depend so much on the type of activity he carries out, as rather on the amount of faith and love that he puts into the carrying out of his service, however humble it may seem.

I am anxious, furthermore, to stress the "complementariness" that exists between your witness and that of the "secular" laity. In fact, the witness of laymen, who live in the world, may be useful to you to remind you that your consecration must not make you indifferent to the salvation of men or to earthly progress, which is also desired by God. On the other hand, the laymen engaged in the world may be beneficially reminded by your witness that earthly progress is not an end in itself.

This puts you, if you permit the expression, at the point at which human realities and ecclesial, the kingdom of man and the kingdom of

God, are welded: with your material tasks on which the smooth operation of the whole community depends, with your apostolic service alongside your priest confreres, with your presence in the world of the school, work, and technology, you are called to carry out a function of connection both within your respective religious families in view of a better organic unity, and in the external world of professions and work, where you can play an extremely important role in helping to bring those environments closer to the Church.

VIEWING ETERNAL THINGS

4. It is clear that the delicacy of such a position also brings risks with it: there is, in fact, always the temptation of losing sight of "eternal things," of "becoming laicized," letting one's vital relations with God cool off and thus losing contact with the source from which the nourishment and support of every activity is derived.

Your work, in fact, is seen to be a living expression of consecration to the Lord only if referred explicitly to him with a consciously renewed resolution of consecrated life. This presupposes, in the first place, a daily revision of life with regard to faithfulness to the commitments undertaken by religious profession. Be generous, beloved sons, in responding to the voice of Christ, who calls you to follow Him closely by means of the practice of poverty, chastity and obedience.

DEEP INTERIOR LIFE

5. Be able, furthermore, to preserve that "primacy of spiritual life" of which the Decree *Perfectae caritatis* speaks (cf. no. 6). Interior life is nourished—it is recalled there—by means of assiduous recourse to the genuine sources of Christian spirituality, which are Holy Scripture and the Liturgy.

In connection with the latter, always remember that conscious participation in liturgical prayer will help you to understand yourselves and the meaning of your presence in the Church more thoroughly. It is necessary to add, however, that such participation would not be possible, in the absence of the habit of personal prayer. Each one must learn to pray also within himself and by himself. Personal devotion, meditation cultivated in the intimacy of one's own spirit, filial and spontaneous conversation with God One and Three, dwelling in the depths of the soul, constitute the premise of truly liturgical prayer.

I wish to indicate another condition for the authenticity of your witness and for its full apostolic efficacy: to offer your cordial and responsible adherence to community life. Living in a religious community is a concrete expression of love for others, and it is a secret of serene and harmonious personal maturation. Acceptance of one's brother, with his qualities and his limitations, the effort to coordinate one's own initiatives with decisions matured together, the self-criticism imposed by continuous confrontation with the evaluations and points of view of others, become not only a very effective training ground of human and Christian virtues, but also a precious opportunity for constant verification of the earnestness with which one endeavors to put into practice in life the obligations assumed in the religious profession.

YOUR SPECIAL MISSION

6. Beloved sons, who spend the best energies of your minds and hearts in the education of youth; and you who care for the sick with brotherly and patient dedication, seeing in them the suffering Christ (cf. Mt. 25:36); and you again who offer your services, as precious as they are humble, alongside your priest confreres, be aware of the special mission entrusted to you by the Lord in the life of His Church.

Learn to cultivate a spirituality which, opening to perception of God's action in the world, will responsibly undertake the task of cooperating in carrying out His plans of salvation. You must endeavor with all the resources of your discernment to grasp the requirements of men, your contemporaries, and then try to meet them with all the riches of your heart. It is up to you to strive to use to advantage all the gifts of your intelligence, in order that your service may be more and more qualified and therefore more worthy of that Jesus, whom you are aware of meeting in every brother, towards whom you go, driven by love.

And be joyful in the daily exercise of your tasks, because it is written that "God loves a cheerful giver'' (2 Cor. 9:7). With this good wish, I entrust the generous resolutions you cherish in your hearts to the motherly intercession of the Blessed Virgin, your special patroness and continual model in the hidden life at Nazareth; and, while I invoke on you and on your work the abundance of heavenly gifts and comforts, I grant to all my apostolic blessing, as a token of my special benevolence.

The Lighted Candles Represent the Mystery of the Liturgy and Your Consecrated Lives

On February 2, 1980, over ten thousand religious men and women took part in the celebration presided over by the Holy Father in the Vatican Basilica on the occasion of the liturgical festivity of the Presentation of the Lord. The traditional offering of blessed candles to the Holy Father by representatives of orders and congregations of religious was renewed on this occasion. John Paul II delivered the following homily.

1. *"Tollite portas...."* "Lift up your heads, O gates! and be lifted up, O ancient doors! that the King of glory may come in" (Ps. 24:7).

There are moments in the liturgy in which these words of the psalmist are heard. Today they seem to speak literally of the gates of the Temple of Jerusalem, its entrances. For He whom the Psalm calls the King of glory, and the prophet Malachi "the messenger of the covenant" (Mal. 3:1), is to enter by these gates. This, therefore, is an unusual moment. The Temple of Jerusalem has existed from the beginning precisely in order that this moment may take place.

Then the psalmist asks: "Who is the King of glory?", and he himself gives the answer: "The Lord, strong and mighty, the Lord, mighty in battle...the Lord of hosts" (Ps. 24:8, 10).

Such is the answer of the psalmist, who speaks with the language of images. The answer of the events, on the other hand, seems to have little to do with the language of the psalmist. In the Gospel of St. Luke we read, in fact, as follows: "And when the time came for their purification according to the law of Moses, they brought him up to Jerusalem to present him to the Lord..." (Lk. 2:22). They brought Him like so many other men obedient to the Law of Israel.... They brought Him to present Him to the Lord. And none of those present could imagine then that the words of the psalmist, the words of the prophet Malachi, were fulfilled at that moment. The child forty days old in His mother's arms had nothing of that "King of glory" about Him. He did not enter the Temple of Jerusalem as "the Lord mighty in battle," as "the strong Lord."

2. And yet, already on that day, Jesus entered the Temple of Israel to announce a particular "battle": a struggle that will be the mission of His life. The struggle, which will end with an unusual triumph. This will be the triumph of the cross, which in the eyes of everyone means not a triumph, but ignominy; not victory, but defeat; and nevertheless it will be a victory.

Precisely what takes place in the Temple of Jerusalem foretells the victory that will be achieved by means of the cross. There takes place, in fact, the rite of consecration to the Lord of Israel of that new Son of Israel, in accordance with what was written in the Law of the Lord: "Every male that opens the womb shall be called holy to the Lord" (Lk. 2:23; cf. Ez. 13:2, 11).

The symbol of this consecration is the offering which, on the occasion of this first visit to the Temple, is made by the parents: "a pair of turtledoves, or two young pigeons" (Lk. 2:24; cf. Lev. 12:8).

This, too, is contained in the norm of the Law.

In this way the people of the Old Covenant wishes to show, in its first-born sons, that it is entirely consecrated to God (Yahweh), its God: that it is His people.

In this case, however, what is taking place is something more than the observance of one of the norms of the Law. If not all those who are present in the Temple realize this, there is one man, however, who is fully aware of the mystery. This man "inspired by the Spirit came into the temple" (Lk. 2:27). He was "righteous and devout...and the Holy Spirit was upon him" (Lk. 2:25). The evangelist writes of him in this way. If, therefore, this man, whose name was Simeon, understood completely the meaning of the event which took place at that moment in the Temple of Jerusalem, he did so because "it had been revealed to him by the Holy Spirit that he should not see death before he had seen Christ the Lord" (Lk. 2:26).

So Simeon sees and announces that the first-born Child, whom Mary and Joseph are offering to God at that moment, is the bearer of a great light, which Israel and the whole of mankind are waiting for: "a light for revelation to the Gentiles and for glory to your people Israel" (Lk. 2:32).

Simeon utters these words in a deep ecstasy. It is the greatest day of his life; after having lived it, he can now tranquilly leave this world. In fact he asks this of God, holding in his arms the Child, whom he has taken from Mary and Joseph: "Lord, now let your servant depart in peace...for my eyes have seen your salvation, which you have prepared in the presence of all peoples" (Lk. 2:29-31).

Thus at the moment of the ritual consecration of the first-born there enters the great announcement of the light and glory, which will expand with the power of the sacrifice. He, in fact, who is now held in old Simeon's arms, is destined to be "a sign that is spoken against" (Lk. 2:34). And this contradiction will be full of suffering which will not spare even the heart of His Mother: "And a sword will pierce through your own soul also" (Lk. 2:35).

When the rite of the consecration of the first-born takes place in the Temple of Jerusalem, the life of Jesus has reached barely forty days. Simeon's words reveal the content of this life up to the end and include the announcement of the cross. This announcement belongs to the fullness of the mystery of the consecration of Jesus in the Temple.

3. You have gathered to take part in today's liturgy, you, dear brothers and sisters, who, by means of religious profession, have dedicated your life completely to God.

This consecration of yours to God, which is complete, definitive and exclusive, is, as it were, a continual growth and a splendid blossoming of that initial consecration, which took place in the sacrament of Baptism; it has its deep roots in it and is a more perfect expression of it (cf. Decree *Perfectae caritatis,* no. 5).

By means of religious profession—as the Dogmatic Constitution *Lumen gentium* affirms —the Christian "consecrates himself wholly to God, his supreme love. In a new and special way he makes himself over to God, to serve and honor Him. True, as a baptized Christian he is dead to sin and dedicated to God; but he desires to derive still more abundant fruit from the grace of his Baptism. For this purpose he makes profession in the Church of the evangelical counsels. He does so for two reasons: first, in order to be set free from hindrances that could hold him back from loving God ardently and worshiping Him perfectly, and secondly, in order to consecrate himself in a more thoroughgoing way to the service of God" (no. 44).

For this reason the feast of the Presentation of the Lord is a special feast for you, consecrated souls, since you participate to an exceptional extent in Christ's donation to the Father, which was announced at the Presentation at the Temple. The offering of your life, which you made joyfully by means of the three vows, finds its constant model, its prize, its encouragement, in the offering of Himself, that the Word of God makes to the Father in His Mother's arms.

4. Simeon utters the words about light before Jesus, at the moment of the Presentation.

Also your lives, beloved brothers and sisters, must be a "light," such as to illuminate the world and temporal reality. In the midst of everything that passes, vanishes and disappears, you, consecrated souls, real sons and daughters of light (cf. Eph. 5:8; 1 Thes. 5:5), must bear truthful witness to future light, to eternal light, to undying light. The Second Vatican Council recalled this to you forcefully: "All the members of the Church should unflaggingly fulfill the duties of their Christian calling. The profession of the evangelical counsels shines before them as a sign which can and should effectively inspire them to do so. For the People of God has here no lasting city but seeks the city which is to come. The religious state of life, in bestowing greater freedom from the cares of earthly existence on those who follow it, simultaneously reveals more clearly to all believers the heavenly goods which are already present in this age, witnessing to the new and eternal life which we have acquired through the redemptive work of Christ and preluding our future resurrection and the glory of the heavenly kingdom" (*Lumen gentium*, no. 44).

The words of Jesus apply to you in a very special way: "Let your light so shine before men, that they may see your good works and give glory to your Father who is in heaven" (Mt. 5:14-16; cf. 1 Pt. 2:12). Yes, brothers and sisters! Let it shine forth, the light of your strong faith; the light of your active charity; the light of your joyful chastity; the light of your generous poverty!

5. How much the Church and the world need this light, this witness!

What an effort we must make in order that its full splendor and its intact eloquence may be realized!

How necessary it is that we should reproduce in ourselves, moral beings, the mystery of Christ's dedication to the Father for the salvation of the world; the dedication which started marvelously with this Presentation at the Temple, the memory of which the whole Church is celebrating today.

How necessary it is that we, too, should fix our eyes on Mary's soul, this soul which, in the words of Simeon, was pierced by a sword that thoughts out of many hearts may be revealed (cf. Lk. 2:35).

Today, dear brothers and sisters, as a sign of that great mystery of the liturgy, and simultaneously of the mystery of your hearts, you present to me the lighted candles. The consecration of the Temple is multiplied, in a way, through the dedication of so many consecrated hearts in the world....

May the thoughts of all these hearts be revealed before the Mother, who knows your consecration and surrounds it with special love.

This Mother is Mary.

This Mother is also the Church.

Amen.

In Your Witness Lies the Vitality of the Catholic School

On Saturday, February 9, 1980, the Holy Father received in audience about eight thousand teachers, pupils and former pupils of the Roman schools "Massimo" and "Santa Maria," which were celebrating respectively the hundredth and the ninetieth anniversary of their foundation. Pope John Paul II delivered the following address.

Beloved brothers and sisters!

"Grace to you and peace from God the Father and the Lord Jesus Christ!" (2 Thes. 1:2)

I am really glad to be able to meet today the superiors, teachers and pupils with the members of their families, of two of the most renowned Catholic schools of Rome: the "Massimo" Institute of the Jesuit Fathers, which has celebrated the first centenary of its foundation, and the "Santa Maria" Institute of the Marianist religious, which remembers its ninetieth anniversary.

These two dates sum up two histories, lived with commitment, enthusiasm, dedication and sacrifice.

...In these hundred years of life, the "Massimo" school has followed the humanistic and Christian program of St. Ignatius and has developed and spread intensely: from the twenty-five pupils of 1879, it has arrived at over one thousand, six hundred.

No less glorious is the history of the ninety years of the "Santa Maria" Institute, run by the sons of the Servant of God Joseph Chaminade, who wished to bring to Rome the experience they had acquired in education at the "College Stanislaus" in Paris and in other educational establishments in Europe and North America: from forty pupils and nine religious in 1889, it has reached one thousand, two hundred and sixty pupils, thirty-six religious and forty-four external teachers in this period.

These figures, beloved brothers and sisters, are eloquent and bear witness effectively and concretely to the dynamism and vitality of your institutes and of what is called the "Catholic" school itself.

...Your institutes are and make a point of proclaiming themselves "Catholic" schools. But what is a Catholic school? What are its main tasks, its specific purposes? The subject is one of such deep and continual topicality that the Second Vatican Council dedicated to these problems a whole document, the Declaration on Christian Education. And this declaration presents, in pregnant synthesis, the threefold characteristic peculiar to Catholic schools, which, like others, pursue cultural purposes and the human formation of the young. "It is, however, the special function of the Catholic school"—the conciliar document affirms—"to develop in the school community an atmosphere animated by a spirit of liberty and charity based on the Gospel. It enables young people, while developing their own personality, to grow at the same time in that new life which has been given them in Baptism. Finally, it so orients the whole of human culture to the message of salvation that the knowledge which the pupils acquire of the world, of life and of men is illumined by faith" (*Gravissimum educationis*, no. 8). This is a text very rich in precious indications, dynamic ferments, and concrete applications. But it is clearly affirmed in it that in the Catholic school it is Christian faith that illuminates knowledge of the whole of reality (world, life, man).

It is true that the school is, as such, the place or the community of learning and culture; but the Catholic school is also, or rather first and foremost, a place and a special community for the education and maturation of faith. I laid special stress on this subject in my recent Apostolic Exhortation on catechesis in our time. A Catholic school—I said—would no longer deserve this title "if, no matter how much it shone for its high level of teaching in non-religious matters, there were justification for reproaching it for negligence or deviation in strictly religious education. Let it not be said that such education will always be given implicitly and indirectly. The special character of the Catholic school, the underlying reason for it, the reason why Catholic parents should prefer it, is precisely the quality of the religious instruction integrated into the education of the pupils" (*Catechesi tradendae*, no. 69). It is the right of pupils of Catholic schools to receive in them a catechesis that is permanent, thorough, articulated, qualified and adapted to the requirements of their age and their cultural preparation. And this religious teaching must be entire in its content, because every disciple of Christ has the right to receive the word of faith in a form that is not mutilated, not distorted, not reduced, but complete and whole, in all its rigor and vigor (cf. *ibid.*, no. 3).

At the center of academic teaching, at the culminating point of interest, must be the Person, the work and the message of Christ: He is our true Teacher (cf. Mt. 23:8-10); He is our way, truth and life (cf. Jn. 14:6); He is our Redeemer and Savior (cf. Eph. 1:7; Col. 1:14). The priority and irreplaceable commitment, both of teachers and of pupils, is to get to know Jesus, by studying, examining and meditating on the Holy Scripture, not as a mere history book, but as the perennial witness of One who is alive, because Jesus rose again and "sits at the right hand side of the Father." Furthermore, when it is a question of Jesus, it is not enough to stop at the plane of theoretical knowledge: His Person, His message continue to challenge us, to involve us, to impel us to live by Him and in Him. Then one is truly a Christian when, day by day, one carries out the requirements, not always easy, of the Gospel of Jesus. Let not the words of St. Augustine be applicable in any way to you, brothers and sisters: "Those who style themselves with a name and do not correspond to it, what good is the name to them if there is not the reality?... In this way, many people call themselves Christians, but are not found to be such in reality, because they are not what they say they are, that is in life, in morals, in hope, in charity" *(In Epist. Joann. tract.* IV, 4: *PL* 35, 2007).

My wish for you, priests and religious, is that in the midst of your dear pupils you may always be joyful witnesses to complete dedication and consecration to God, and that you consider it a real honor, as well as a serious duty, to transmit and communicate the Christian faith to them in the teaching of religion. But let your evangelical life be a living and luminous catechesis for the boys and youths entrusted to your educational apostolate.

My wish for you, lay teachers, is that you may live intensely the sense of responsibility of teaching in a Catholic school. In this way your pupils will appreciate you and love you not only for your specific professional and cultural competence, but above all for your Christian consistency.

My wish for you, fathers and mothers, rightly concerned about the cultural preparation, but even more about the human, civil and religious formation of your sons, is that you may always be aware that you are the first true and irreplaceable educators of your children! Always follow them with that extraordinary love, which God the Father has sown in your heart! Learn to understand them, listen to them, guide them!

And today at this meeting, charged with promises and enthusiasm, what will the Pope say to you, beloved students, who are the real protagonists of the school? You are the point of convergence of the affection, cares and interest of your parents, your teachers, your superiors. Respond to this sum of love with a constant commitment for your human, cultural and Christian maturation. Prepare, in serious and assiduous study, for the tasks that divine Providence has in store for you tomorrow within civil society and the ecclesial community. The future of the nation, nay more of the world, depends on you! The society of the future will be the one constructed by you; and you are already constructing it, in these years, in your classrooms, at your meetings, in your associations.

May the Pope be able to repeat to you too, with joy, the words that St. John addressed to the young: "I write to you, young men, because you are strong, and the word of God abides in you, and you have overcome the evil one" (1 Jn. 2:14).

Yes, beloved young people! Be strong in the faith; let Christ, the Incarnate Word of God, direct your lives; in this way you will overcome evil, which is manifested in selfishness, divisions, hatred and violence!

My apostolic blessing to everyone!

Church Proclaims the Ideal of Vocation

On February 16, 1980, the Holy Father received in audience members of the National Council and the Regional Secretaries for Vocations, and delivered the following address.

Beloved brothers!

I am sincerely glad to be able to meet, even if briefly, you members of the National Council and Regional Secretaries for Vocations, gathered in Rome in these days to meditate together on problems concerning vocational promotion, sponsored by the Italian Conference of Major Superiors.

1. I must tell you, in the first place, of my deep satisfaction and my fatherly encouragement for our specific pastoral commitment, a difficult and delicate one—it is true—but highly meritorious with regard to the whole Church.

Religious vocation, like priestly vocation, is an admirable gift, which Christ bestowed on His Bride and which she, therefore, must keep and preserve with jealous love. For this purpose the whole Church is committed to praying constantly, keeping watch assiduously, and proclaiming with faith the eternal value of complete and definitive consecration to God, to multiplying her own generosity in order to spread the ideal of vocation, lived in constant practice of the evangelical counsels of chastity, poverty and obedience, so that there will be no lack, in the harmonious development of the Mystical Body, of men and women who, in monasteries, or in schools, in hospitals, or in the missions, honor the Bride of Christ, and offer generous and extremely varied services to all men, with perseverance and humble faithfulness to their consecration (cf. *Lumen gentium*, no. 46).

CHRIST'S INVITATION

2. Certainly, to live fully the requirements of the religious or priestly vocation, a constant spirit of sacrifice and lasting self-mastery are necessary. But it is worthwhile to face these difficulties in order to respond with ardent generosity to the invitation of Jesus: "Follow me!" (cf. Mt. 19:21; Lk. 18:22) Has this capacity of dedication to Jesus diminished in the men and women of our time? I think that we are all convinced that the men and women of today, and in particular the young, have such a need of truth, justice, love, solidarity and ideals, so as to make them ready to live in depth the exalting experience of religious vocation.

And the common desire is that there may be many of them who follow Christ's invitation, remembering the words of St. Augustine: *Non sitis pigri qui potestis, quibus adspira Deus apprehendere gradus meliores.... Aspice eum qui te ducit, et non respicies retro, unde te educit. Qui te ducit, ante te ambulat; unde te educit, post te est. Ama ducentem...* ("Do not be negligent, you who have the power, you whom God calls to ascend higher.... Look at the one who is guiding you and do not look backwards, from where he is taking you away. He who guides you, walks in front of you; the place from which he is taking you away is behind you. Love the one who is guiding you....": *Enarr. in Psal.* 76, 16: *PL* 36, 368f.).

TO FAITHFUL RELIGIOUS

3. Concluding this short meeting of ours, I wish to address ideally all religious and priests who are living their vocation serenely, day after day, faithful to the commitments assumed, humble and hidden constructors of the kingdom of God, from whose words, behavior and lives there shines forth the luminous joy of the choice made. It is precisely such religious and priests who, by means of their example, will spur so many to accept the charism of vocation in their hearts. I remind them of what the Second Vatican Council recommended: "Let religious see well to it that the Church truly shows forth Christ through them with ever-increasing clarity to believers and unbelievers alike—Christ in contemplation on the mountain, or proclaiming the kingdom of God to the multitudes, or healing the sick and maimed and converting sinners to a good life, or blessing children and doing good to all men, always in obedience to the will of the Father who sent Him" (cf. *Lumen gentium,* no. 46).

May my apostolic blessing accompany you always in your ministry and make it fruitful with good for the Church.

Lent: the Time of Conversion

On Sunday, March 2, 1980, the Holy Father delivered the following address to the thousands of faithful present in St. Peter's Square for the recitation of the Angelus. The following is an excerpt.

In the period of Lent the Church prays for vocations, priestly and religious. This is a problem of which it is not possible to think in any other way than by appealing to grace, the fullness of which is in the crucified and risen Christ.

All of us pray that the ecclesiastical seminaries and novitiates may be filled, that the individual Churches, and also communities— parishes and religious congregations—may be able to look to the future confidently, certain that there will be no lack of those laborers, whom the Lord sends out "into his harvest" (Mt. 9:38); that there will be no lack of priests, who, dedicating themselves "exclusively" to the kingdom of God, will celebrate the Eucharist, preach the Word of the Lord and carry out the pastoral ministry; that there will be no lack of persons, men and women, capable of complete dedication of their lives to the divine Bridegroom in the spirit of poverty, chastity and obedience in witness "to the future world," impelled to do so by unlimited love of their neighbor.

We all pray in order that the young, boys and girls, may discover within themselves the grace of vocation, as a special gift for the Church, a gift that Christ Himself grafts onto their hearts; and that they may follow this call without looking back (cf. Lk. 9:62) and without being afraid of their own weakness, of the spirit of this world, and of the "prince of darkness."

If we pray for this, then we are certain: the Lord of the harvest will answer our request if we show complete obedience to Christ according to the words that rang out on the Mount of the Transfiguration:

"This is my Son, my Chosen; listen to him!" (Lk. 9:35)

In no other way. In no other way. So we cannot harbor in secret suspicions or doubts about the essence of the ministerial priesthood, about the rightness of the centuries-old practice of our Church, which unites priesthood with availability to serve Christ and the Church "with an undivided heart." We cannot doubt the power of Christ, the work of His grace. We must think to the very end together with Him, accepting that what seems impossible for men, is, however, possible for God (cf. Mt. 19:26).

So it is necessary to pray for vocations and it is necessary to pray trusting unlimitedly, unreservedly for this grace, the fullness of which is in Christ, the beloved Son of the Father. To pray in this way, means to be converted. Lent is a time of conversion.

Prayer, Support and Nourishment of Consecrated Religious Living

The Holy Father, not being able to receive participants in the plenary session of the Sacred Congration for Religious and for Secular Institutes on March 7, 1980, owing to a slight attack of influenza, sent them a message, entrusting the Cardinal Secretary of State to read it on his behalf.

His Eminence Cardinal Agostino Casaroli went to the headquarters of the above Congregation at 12:30 and read the following text.

Lord Cardinals and venerated brothers!

1. "Grace to you and peace from God our Father and the Lord Jesus Christ" (Rom. 1:7). With these words of the Apostle Paul I wish to give you my greeting.

You have wished to send me the testimony not only of the sincere affection—so willingly returned!—that binds you to the Vicar of Christ, but also of the will that has sustained your work in these days, with the aim of bringing it about that religious men and women in the world, by means of faithful adherence to the teachings of the Gospel, may live in deeper and deeper communion with the Church.

Expressing to you my gratitude for this commitment, I am happy to confirm to you, in the first place, my convinced appreciation for what the specific charism of religious life represents in the structure of the Mystical Body. It is a great treasure in the Church: without religious orders, without consecrated life, the Church would not be fully herself.

In fact, the profession of the evangelical counsels makes it possible for those who have received this special gift to conform more deeply to that life of chastity, poverty and obedience, which Christ chose for Himself and which Mary, His Mother and Mother of the Church, embraced (cf. Apostolic Exhortation *Evangelica testificatio,* no. 2), as a typological model for the Church herself. At the same time, this profession is a very special testimony of the constant search for God and absolute dedication to the growth of the kingdom, to which Christ invites those who believe in Him (cf. Mt. 6:33). Without this concrete sign, the "salt" of faith would run the risk of being diluted in a world that is being secularized, such as the present one (cf. *ibid.,* no. 3).

PERFECTING CHARITY

It is clear that, to remain faithful to their consecration to the Lord and to be able to offer a visible testimony of it, religious must perfect their charity, in the dialogue of prayer with God. To keep perception of the value of consecrated life quite clear, a deep vision of faith is necessary, and this is sustained and nourished by means of prayer.

The subject chosen for this plenary meeting must, therefore, be considered of prime importance and I am certain that from this meeting of yours there will derive for all religious a precious encouragement to persevere in the commitment of bearing witness before the world to the primacy of man's relationship with God. Strengthened by the indications, which will spring from your meeting in Rome, they will not fail to dedicate, with renewed conviction, a sufficiently long time to pauses of prayer before the Lord, to tell Him their love and, above all, to feel loved by Him.

Without prayer, religious life loses its meaning and does not reach its purpose. The incisive words of the Apostolic Exhortation *Evangelica testificatio* make us reflect: "Do not forget the witness of history: faithfulness to prayer or its abandonment are the model of the vitality or decadence of religious life" (no. 42).

SILENCE AND DISCIPLINE

2. During these days, you have made an effort to study deeply the value of contemplation, on the one hand, and, on the other, the opportune ways to immerse the religious life more and more into it. In the case of religious of apostolic life, it will be a question of promoting integration between interiority and activity. Their first duty, in fact, is that of being with Christ. A constant danger for apostolic workers is to become so much involved in their own work for the Lord, as to forget the Lord of all work.

It will be necessary, therefore, for them to become increasingly aware of the importance of *prayer* in their lives and to learn to dedicate themselves to it generously (cf. Apostolic Exhortation *Evangelica testificatio*, no. 45). To arrive at this, they need the silence of their whole being, and this calls for areas of *actual silence* and personal discipline, to facilitate contact with God.

Participation in the *Liturgy of the Church* (Divine Office, sacramental life) is a very special means of contemplation, especially at the climax of the *Eucharistic Sacrifice*, in which inner prayer mingles with exterior worship. The commitment to take part in it daily will help religious renew daily the offering of themselves to the Lord.

Gathered in the Lord's name, religious communities have the Eucharist as their natural center; it is natural, therefore, that they should be visibly assembled round an oratory, in which the presence of the Blessed Sacrament expresses and realizes what must be the principal mission of every religious family (cf. Apostolic Exhortation *Evangelica testificatio*, no. 48).

Religious houses must, therefore, be above all oases of prayer and meditation, places of personal and community dialogue with Him who is and must remain the first and principal interlocutor of their days, so full of work. Superiors must not be afraid, therefore, of reminding their confreres often that a pause of real worship is more fruitful and rich than any other activity, even if intense, and of an apostolic character. In fact, "no movement in religious life has any importance unless it be also movement inwards to the 'still center' of your existence, where Christ is. It is not what you *do* that matters most; but what you *are,* as women consecrated to God" (Address to priests, religious men and women at Maynooth: October 1, 1979).

The contemplative life of religious would be incomplete if it were not directed to filial love towards her who is the Mother of the Church and of consecrated souls. This love for the Virgin will be manifested with the celebration of her feasts, and in particular with daily prayers in her honor, particularly the rosary. The daily recitation of the rosary is a centuries-old tradition for religious and so it is not useless to recall the opportuneness, fragrance and efficacy of this prayer, which proposes to our meditation the mysteries of the Lord's life.

ROLE OF CONTEMPLATIVES

3. I know that in the context of your work you have devoted special attention to souls consecrated to contemplative life, recognizing in them one of the most precious treasures of the Church. Docile to the invitation of the Divine Master, they have chosen the good portion (cf. Lk. 10:42), that is, prayer, silence, contemplation, exclusive love of God and complete dedication to His service. They must know that the Church relies a great deal on their spiritual contribution.

In the Decree *Perfectae caritatis* the Second Vatican Council did not confine itself to affirming that the contemplative institutes keep, today too, a fully valid meaning and function; it said that the place they occupy in the Mystical Body is an "honored" one (*praeclara pars*). For contemplatives "offer to God an exceptional sacrifice of praise," they lend luster to God's people with "abundant fruits of holiness," they "sway them by their example," and they "enlarge the Church by their hidden apostolic fruitfulness" (cf. no. 7).

Certainly, the requirements raised for the Church by evangelization today are multiple and urgent. It would be a mistake, however, to consider, on the basis of the necessities, also urgent ones, of the apostolate today, a form of life dedicated exclusively to contemplation as a thing of the past. The Council Fathers, tackling in the Decree *Ad gentes* the problem of the proclamation of the Good News to all men, wished on the contrary to stress the effective contribution of contemplatives to apostolic work (cf. no. 40). They expressed the hope that, in the young Churches, among the various forms of religious life, there will also be the constitution of communities of contemplative life, to guarantee "the fullness of the Church's presence" (cf. no. 18).

TOTALITY OF COMMITMENT

Is it not significant, moreover, to point out, looking back on the history of the Church, that it is precisely in the centuries in which the necessities of evangelization were greatest, that contemplative life had an almost miraculous blossoming and expansion? Should we not see in that an indication of the Spirit, who reminds us all, often tempted by the promptings of efficiency, of the supremacy of supernatural means over purely human ones?

So I turn my eyes confidently towards these souls dedicated with totality of commitment to contemplation, and I entrust to the ardor of their charity the harassing cares of the universal ministry, which has been entrusted to me. I know how attached they are to their special vocation, how joyfully they accept its requirements of daily sacrifice, how they are able to give a place in their prayer to the work, the sorrows and the hopes of their contemporaries. My hope is that they will study more and more deeply, in order to live it more and more intensely, the spirituality of their Founders, without letting themselves be tempted by more fashionable methods or techniques, the inspiration of which has often little to do with the Gospel. The contemplative and mystical heritage of the Church is exceptionally vast and deep: it is necessary, therefore, to take care that all monasteries will undertake to get to know it, cultivate it and teach it.

It will be very helpful in order to attain these purposes for enclosure to be observed with rightful rigor, in accordance with the Second Vatican Council which spoke out in favor of its maintenance (cf. Decree *Perfectae caritatis*, no. 16). In fact, the abandonment of enclosure would mean loss of what is specific in one of the forms of religious life, with which the Church manifests to the world the preeminence of contemplation over action, of what is eternal over what is temporal. Enclosure does not "isolate" contemplative souls from the communion of the Mystical Body. It puts them, on the contrary, at the heart of the Church, as my predecessor, Pope Paul VI, rightly affirmed, adding that these souls "nourish the spiritual riches of the Church, exalt her prayer, sustain her charity, share her sufferings, her toils, her apostolate, her hopes, and increase her merits" (Address of February 2, 1966).

STRENGTH FROM CONTEMPLATION

4. There is furthermore a particular problem, the importance of which deserves to be mentioned today: that of the close relations between religious institutes and the clergy with regard to the contemplative dimension that every life dedicated to the Lord must have, as its fundamental element.

Secular priests need to draw from contemplation the strength and support of their apostolate. As in the past, they must normally find backing, in this connection, in experienced religious and in contact with monasteries, ready to receive them for spiritual exercises and for periods of meditation and renewal.

On their side, religious must be able to find in the clergy, confessors and spiritual directors, capable of giving them help to understand and put into practice their consecration in a better way. The influence of priests is, moreover, very often a determinant in encouraging the discovery and subsequent development of the religious vocation.

It is necessary, therefore, that the clergy and religious, and in particular the bishops and superiors, should endeavor to find, for the important problem of the interdependence of the two states, a solution adapted to the times in which we live.

I would also like to add a reference to the new forms of contemplative life, which are emerging here and there in the Church and in which one or other element of spiritual life is stressed. They are all interesting experiments and the Church follows them benevolently and attentively.

What I am anxious to recall is that these experiments must not weaken, however, in any way attachment and faithfulness to the forms of contemplative life, tested by centuries of history: they remain true sources of prayer and reliable schools of holiness, the fruitfulness of which has never been belied.

CONTINUAL APPRENTICESHIP

5. Beloved brothers, religious life does not have a definitive goal in this life: it is a gift in continual development and a progress towards more and more noble aims. In this sense, St. Benedict affirmed that the monk's life is a continual apprenticeship for the Lord's service: *dominici schola servitii* (*Rule*, prol.). A school, in which the interior Teacher is the Spirit.

In the course of these days, you have sought to listen to this silent and sweet Teacher, to gather His suggestions faithfully and express their interior light in concrete norms. May your work produce abundant fruit, offering all religious opportune help to carry out what the Lord expects of them, to the advantage of the whole Christian community.

With this hope and invoking the motherly protection of the Blessed Virgin, the peerless model of complete consecration, I willingly send you my special blessing, which I am happy to extend to all the souls that, in chastity, poverty and obedience, are endeavoring to follow already in this life "the Lamb, wherever he goes" (cf. Rev. 14:4).

The Value of Contemplation for the Grace of Vocations

The Pope's meeting with the sisters of the dioceses of Spoleto and Norcia and of the other dioceses of Umbria took place in the early afternoon of March 23, 1980, in St. Benedict's Basilica in Norcia. Pope John Paul II delivered the following address.

In the series of meetings on this extraordinary day, it gives me special consolation to find myself with sisters of various Benedictine convents in neighboring regions of Italy.

I greet with equal affection all sisters belonging to other orders and institutes for the act of filial respect they have wished to pay me.

This qualified presence, while it makes more joyful the beginning of the celebrations of the fifteenth centenary of the birth of St. Benedict, offers the Pope who has come to venerate his birthplace the opportunity to recall some principles of Benedictine spirituality, from which so many religious families have been able to benefit in the course of the centuries. Right from the beginning, in fact, it left a track, a reliable path for monastic and religious life, arousing holy enthusiasm in generous souls which have always sought inspiration in it. Also at present, with its main element, namely contemplation, it is destined to kindle in minds and hearts open to the influence of the grace of vocation ardor to ascend the spiritual heights.

SCHOOLS OF GOD'S SERVICE

1. I look, therefore, with sincere admiration to all the convents of the Benedictine sisters, and with deep satisfaction I use in their regard the image dear to St. Benedict, who considered them "schools of God's service."

I also think with gratification of all the houses of women religious which are found all over this Umbrian region, docile as it has always been down the centuries to the inspiring calls of the Spirit. You, beloved sisters, desire nothing else but to devote yourselves to God with purity of heart, in solitude, silence and prayer: mental prayer and choral prayer *opus cui nihil praeferendum,* in pursuit of the holy aim that there should not enter your spirit, nor that there should leave it, anything that is not "deiform" and that does not lead to God.

In your hermitages the most important choice of your life has been made through your resolution: you have generously renounced every thing or attraction that the world could give you. You have detached yourselves from all earthly affections in order to unite yourselves exclusively to God and possess Him permanently in your hearts.

At this height of mystical life, which is the essence of perfection, absorbed "in contemplative thoughts" (Dante, *Par.* XXI, 117), you are given the privilege of experiencing, tasting and hearing God, by means of the continual application of spiritual powers, even if in the darkness of faith And you know by experience that the more intimate the conversation with the heavenly Father, the more one feels that the time for this lofty act of charity is never sufficient.

How could I fail to recall, in this connection, the intense day spent by the two saints, brother and sister, in praise of God and in holy conversation? As St. Gregory the Great tells us, it was followed by the famous nocturnal vigil obtained at the request of St. Scholastica, so that the two saints spent that whole night satiating themselves with sweet talks and telling each other of their experience of spiritual life (*Dialogues*, 2, 33; *PL* 66, 194-196).

MONUMENT OF WISDOM AND TOPICAL INTEREST

2. The golden rule, dictated by the holy patriarch, has been, and still is, a stimulus to foster contemplative life and sustain its persevering commitment. It was considered by all subsequent legislators a monument of wisdom and perennial topical interest, because its teachings offer the guarantee of certainty, fruitfulness and clarity since they derive from St. Benedict's perfect adherence to the Gospel and to the magisterium of the Church.

Those prescriptions, ordained in such a way as to put God and Christ at the center of the universe and to affirm their absolute primacy over all things, could not have described more effectively the spiritual path of the Benedictine sister. They have been a source of inspiration also for so many other souls, eager to dedicate themselves completely to God and their brothers.

Habitually available for God through sanctifying grace, the Benedictine sister is led to view herself in the presence of her Lord, her only love and good, with extreme sincerity and truth, and she must carry out her own interior and exterior activity in this situation. This presupposes a resolute and constant aspiration to conform her own will to that of God. St. Benedict foresaw this. In his Rule, in fact, there is a continual call to obedience as the most appropriate virtue to reach holiness.

3. While I invite you, beloved sisters in Christ, to keep faith with the prescriptions and charisms of your founders and foundresses, I wish to express to you the gratitude of the Church for the activity you carry out on her behalf.

Not only, indeed, do you offer God an excellent sacrifice of praise, and with very abundant fruits of holiness honor the People of God and move it by your example (cf. *Perfectae caritatis*, no. 7), but you carry out with your life of hidden sacrifice an act of propitiation of the Father of Mercies, on behalf of the Church, in the difficulties she is passing through at the present time.

In particular, beloved sisters in Christ, I am relying on this precious collaboration today, when the Italian Church, gathered in prayer, presents to the Lord her suffering because of the moral and social order so deeply disturbed by destruction and terrorism, because of the many victims who have paid with their lives for faithfulness to their duty and to the ideals of human and civil society, and because of the desolation of so many relatives deprived of their most legitimate affections. The passion of Christ, which we are preparing to relive in the days of Holy Week, now approaching, continues in the 'suffering and blood of these brothers and sisters of ours, struck down by murderous hatred. The Church weeps for them, while she weeps over the wounds of her Lord.

Hoping that all forms of violence will at last be banished and that justice and peace will be reached by means of reason and mutual understanding, I ask you to offer your supplication, strengthened by special and intimate sacrifices, to Christ the Lord today, in order that innate goodness, serene activity and human and civil cohesion—the fruit of exemplary and consistent Christian morals—may triumph in the beloved Italian nation.

To your continual offering, which supplicates, worships and placates the divine Majesty, I entrust the Church and I entrust my universal intentions as Pastor and Father.

In my turn I entrust you to Mary, the Virgin, the model of contemplative and active souls, the Mother of the Church, and I leave my blessing to you, extending it to one and all of the sisters in your institutes, as well as to the respective members of your families.

INDEX

Fidelity and Relevance

Compiled by the Daughters
   of St. Paul

What religious community or what individual religious is not searching for reliable, clear guidelines in these days of confusion? And to what more reliable source can we turn than to the Vicar of Christ? Hence this volume with over 325 selected passages from Pope Paul's talks. The challenge of Vatican II to adapt and renew religious life is looked at in its myriad aspects: its essence, interior quality, and dynamics. 246 pages
paper $2.75 — SP0160

Religious Life Today

John A. Hardon, SJ

Twelve penetrating lectures on the nature of authentic religious life and the role of religious in today's world. 176 pages
cloth $3.00; paper $2.00 — SP0610

That Christ May Live in Me

J. Alberione, SSP, STD

"Christian, religious and priestly perfection lies in this: to establish ourselves totally in Jesus Master, Way, Truth and Life. Indeed this is the way to reach the supreme height of our personality: I who think in Jesus Christ, I who love in Jesus Christ, I who will in Jesus Christ. Or: Christ who thinks in me, who loves in me, who wills in me."

—Father James Alberione

In these penetrating reflections of Father James Alberione on Jesus the Divine Master, we find ourselves before a man profoundly formed by the Word of God. We find a man steeped in the Trinity, of which Jesus Master is, at the same time, revealer and way. To be in Christ is to be in the Trinity. For this reason imitation and discipleship become very pressing and urgent.

170 pages; cloth $3.50; paper $2.25 — SP0742

Daughters of St. Paul

IN MASSACHUSETTS
    50 St. Paul's Ave. Jamaica Plain, Boston, MA 02130;
        617-522-8911; 617-522-0875;
    172 Tremont Street, Boston, MA 02111; **617-426-5464;**
        617-426-4230
IN NEW YORK
    78 Fort Place, Staten Island, NY 10301; **212-447-5071**
    59 East 43rd Street, New York, NY 10017; **212-986-7580**
    7 State Street, New York, NY 10004; **212-447-5071**
    625 East 187th Street, Bronx, NY 10458; **212-584-0440**
    525 Main Street, Buffalo, NY 14203; **716-847-6044**
IN NEW JERSEY
    Hudson Mall — Route 440 and Communipaw Ave.,
        Jersey City, NJ 07304; **201-433-7740**
IN CONNECTICUT
    202 Fairfield Ave., Bridgeport, CT 06604; **203-335-9913**
IN OHIO
    2105 Ontario St. (at Prospect Ave.), Cleveland, OH 44115; **216-621-9427**
    25 E. Eighth Street, Cincinnati, OH 45202; **513-721-4838**
IN PENNSYLVANIA
    1719 Chestnut Street, Philadelphia, PA 19103; **215-568-2638**
IN FLORIDA
    2700 Biscayne Blvd., Miami, FL 33137; **305-573-1618**
IN LOUISIANA
    4403 Veterans Memorial Blvd., Metairie, LA 70002; **504-887-7631;**
        504-887-0113
    1800 South Acadian Thruway, P.O. Box 2028, Baton Rouge, LA 70821
        504-343-4057; 504-343-3814
IN MISSOURI
    1001 Pine Street (at North 10th), St. Louis, MO 63101; **314-621-0346;**
        314-231-5522
IN ILLINOIS
    172 North Michigan Ave., Chicago, IL 60601; **312-346-4228**
IN TEXAS
    114 Main Plaza, San Antonio, TX 78205; **512-224-8101**
IN CALIFORNIA
    1570 Fifth Avenue, San Diego, CA 92101; **714-232-1442**
    46 Geary Street, San Francisco, CA 94108; **415-781-5180**
IN HAWAII
    1143 Bishop Street, Honolulu, HI 96813; **808-521-2731**
IN ALASKA
    750 West 5th Avenue, Anchorage AK 99501; **907-272-8183**
IN CANADA
    3022 Dufferin Street, Toronto 395, Ontario, Canada
IN ENGLAND
    57, Kensington Church Street, London W. 8, England
IN AUSTRALIA
    58 Abbotsford Rd., Homebush, N.S.W., Sydney 2140, Australia